the Book of Mormon
speaks for itself

We Explore to Discover
What This Book
Says for Itself

BOOK OF MORMON

the Book of Mormon speaks for itself By Roy A. Cheville

The Department of Christian Education

Reorganized Church of Jesus Christ of Latter Day Saints

Jacket design by John Livesay

Read This First!

This section of a book usually is called the foreword. Here let us consider it a foundation word. This sets forth the way we shall be looking with and living with the Book of Mormon.

Here is the intent of this introductory study of ours: We shall get into the book itself and let it speak in its way. We shall look and listen and live with.

We shall also endeavor to discover its message for living in our day. A book of merit speaks out of its own world, in its own way, but it has continuing application. If the Book of Mormon has worth, it must have something to say that will contribute to living in contemporary times.

In many cases when we encounter a book that has provoked discussion, we are inclined to assemble materials about it. We may consult encyclopedias, read press releases, run through synopses and summaries. This can be helpful and contributive, but it has limitations. We need to catch something of the soul and voice of the book.

Early in my university studies I came upon the writings of Paul Tillich. He was still in Germany. Later I read some of his books. I saw him as a philosopher in the field of religion. I got hold of some of his phrasings. I heard disciples quote him. As yet he was mainly concepts and postulates. Then I turned to the man himself. His thinking was an integral part of him and could not be separated from him, but he was more than phrases and quotations. One day I met him and caught something of the graciousness and the depth of his personhood. One weekend shortly after his death I stayed alone in the apartment where he and Mrs. Tillich lived, near the University of Chicago. In my limited way I lived with this noble man. I began to sense how many admirers got hold of concepts and conclusions without catching the spirit of the man himself. I caught something of his adventuring life.

This approach to "knowing" applies to books; certainly it applies to the Book of Mormon. This is no ordinary book. It cannot be written off with others. Its claims are extraordinary. Said one, "If only part of what this book claims is true, it still is really something." Another commented, "They say Joe Smith wrote it. I don't think he had what it took to put this together." Spoke another, "What the book says is all right, but I wish that whoever wrote it had had some journalistic style." Such comments ought to make our exploration appealing. They need not make us defensive or argumentative.

There is a wide range of attitudes toward the Book of Mormon. Some have unquestioning acceptance. Some look at it with agnostic denunciation. A firm believer in the monopoly of the Bible burst out, "It is sacrilegious to pawn off another book for scriptures." Such diversity ought to add to the appeal of the book.

The diversity in the company of those who accept the Book of Mormon as scripture is much the same as that found among believers in the Bible. Some consider it inerrant, the very word of God. These believe that it is to be interpreted "literally" and that no word is to be changed. There are those who affirm that it is necessary to see it in terms of the times and the thought worlds out of which the writings came to be. These see relativity in inspiration applying to writing, translating, interpreting. These look for improved, clearer phrasing. A difference is that there are no ancient manuscripts to be used in research about the Book of Mormon.

There is diversity, too, in concepts about the functioning of divine inspiration in producing scriptures. Some believe that when a person is inspired by the Spirit, God takes over and the inspired person becomes a passive instrument through which God operates. Others consider that the Spirit of God functions through the natural and cultivated resources of the person, "quickening" and directing them. In this latter view the individuality and resources of the person are utilized. Each writer has his own imagery, his own linguistic resources, his own conceptual world, and God speaks through these. Sooner or later these diverse concepts about the workings of the Holy Spirit in the inspiring of persons must be considered in relation to the Book of Mormon.

Some supporters of the book scarcely get into the story. They become so intent on "proving" that it is "of God" that they scarcely delve into the book itself. Some of them quote passages from the Old Testament to indicate that such a book was to "come forth." Some draw on Latin-American archaeology for their "proof." Some narrate how the Book of Mormon was produced in the early nineteenth century through "the gift and power of God." From these fields can come assisting data, but these cannot take the place of permitting the book to speak for itself.

This foundation word calls us to get hold of the intent and motivation of the writers. When we understand this, we come to sense why some things were said and why they were said as they were. For instance, some readers get tired of the emphasis on record keeping in the Book of Mormon. This seems legalistic. As we explore, we see that these migrants to a new land brought their scriptures and kept their own records as a part of their Hebrew heritage. They believed that this would insure them against spiritual illiteracy and lack of spiritual foundations. When we catch this concern we understand the emphasis on records.

Some examiners of the Book of Mormon as well as other scriptures consider literary criticism, textual materials, historical foundations, but never use the scriptures functionally in the business of living. They do not validate the book in the laboratory of living.

In this survey exploration we shall get into the Book of Mormon itself. We want to find out what it has to say in its own way with a view to discovering how it can guide, counsel, inspire us in living "together with God" here and now.

This is basic. Let's have the book speak for itself! And we shall look and listen to find what God is saying to us.

Roy A. Cheville

Twelve Explorations into the Book of Mormon to discover what it speaks.

Exploration I. Scriptures Speak Their Own Language . . . Scriptures speak in ways distinctive to them. Each speaks as God's voice. This book has ancient Hebrew content and aura. It speaks as extension of Hebrew faith.

The Book of Mormon says it is a compilation of scriptural writings. It says these writings came out of ancient America. It says the people who produced these writings came out of what we now call the Near East, most of them from the region of Jerusalem. It says these people came to be some of the forerunners of the people Columbus found and called Indians. It says these original peoples broke into hostile camps. The story says that the darker-skinned people survived. It says that the record was kept for the teaching, guiding, and converting of the descendants of these survivors and for all peoples of the world. This book says that Jesus Christ came to this Western land in ancient times, just after rounding out his ministry in Judea and Galilee.

This Book of Mormon says that it is to stand beside the Bible as the voice of God to men of all times. This is a daring claim. This claim stands out as more daring when we are aware that the book came off the press in

1830 when the idea that there would be any scriptures other than the Bible was denounced as horrible heresy. Yes, this book says it is scripture, directed by God.

It is expedient to examine how persons look at what they consider scripture. We see that they do not look with the same view, in the same mood. This applies to the Old Testament and the New Testament. Let us ask how we are going to open the book so it can speak for itself. We shall need to learn how to listen in the language of the book. We want to discover what the book has to say in its own way.

Scriptures Have Been Selected

In the larger sense "scripture" denotes what is written. In the field of religion, however, there is a more restricted meaning. Influenced by time and use and decisions of leaders, councils have selected certain writings and have decreed that they speak for God. There has been a general tendency to make the chosen writings rather restricted. Those chosen are called a canon. Any new writings have had a hard time getting on the canon list. In most cases there has been little chance of approval or confirmation. The Book of Mormon encounters this resistance on the part of Bible believers.

As soon as a thing is written down, something seems to happen to it. It assumes a there-it-is quality. It can be referred to as definite. It can be quoted as proof. If what is written down is received as "coming on good authority," it can become proof text and final word. In this spirit the ancients would say, "It is written." The truly devout could say, "God has spoken." So through the centuries the term "scripture" has come to refer to the writings characterized as sacred and authoritative. In the Hebrew and Christian tradition this has meant that God has had something to do with their coming to be. Moslems claim that Allah provided their Koran.

Axiomatic Authority

An axiom is not questioned. It is presumed to carry its own credentials. For centuries the Bible carried this axiomatic authority. It had scriptural monopoly. During recent decades the Bible has been increasingly examined. Those who have looked at the Bible as "the very inerrant word of God" have resisted and denounced this examining and questioning concerning what the Bible is, how it came to be, and what it says. They cling to inherited beliefs, attitudes, and values. Any newcomer-pretender such as the Book of Mormon is denounced and discarded without examination. The Bible is there. It stands on its own merits. They consider it disruptive and heretical to ask questions concerning that which came from God. True axiomatic believers would think and say, "Where the scriptures speak, we speak," and, further, "Where the scriptures speak, God speaks."

At such times there arise those who stand at the opposite pole. These find a kind of satisfaction and delight in going to the other extreme. They tend to push their examining to the limit. Often they are inclined to be cynical and negative. Such persons are wont to state what they do not believe rather than what they do believe. They point out what is wrong with prevailing beliefs rather than state what they do believe. These usually call into question the axioms that have been presumed about scriptures.

The "axiomats" and the non-axiomats stand out in sharp contrast. The former are inclined to say, "Listen as the Bible speaks!" Then they make the Bible say what they want the Bible to say and this becomes what God has said. With presumptions about the unchanging nature of God, these believers affirm that what he once said he duplicates today. Therefore, there is no need for God to be speaking anew. The basic axioms are to stand and to provide foundation.

God Speaks in Available Language

The truly perceptive person has great empathy for God in his speaking. The concern is not about God's ability but about the resources available to God for speaking clearly to man in view of man's limited resources in language expression. Whenever God speaks to humans, He is conditioned by the human resources for thinking, for speaking. And if God were to employ some celestial medium of communication, man would have to be schooled to apprehend what God was saying. By the time man could understand the message, the stream of life would have moved on.

Awareness of this prompts us to improve and increase our language resources for thinking, speaking, writing. The competent believer in continuing revelation is concerned with developing himself so that he and God can communicate with increasing clarity and richness. There is fitness in the prayer of a man who sensed this conditioning factor: "God, help me to grow in thinking, in speaking, so you will have a better chance to say to me what you want to say."

Inspiration Quickens Our Language Potential

Inspiration does not weaken or devaluate personhood. Rather inspiration, prompted by God through his Holy Spirit, increases, refines, and utilizes man's personhood.

God is calling every man to discover and develop his own personal potential and to devote this potential in co-working with Him. The ideal for inspiration is not using a non-thinking Balaam's ass to issue sounds the animal does not understand. The ideal is rather in the counsel expressed to Oliver Cowdery when he was directed to use his powers, to think things through, and God would quicken these powers and confirm the insights that were sound and fruitful. This places a premium on developing resources for perceiving and speaking what God says. God is thereby enabled to say more and more as we develop more and more in communicative resources and skills and understandings.

Conditioning Factors in Writing What God Wants to Say

When we pick up a book of scriptures and explore to find its message, we are involved in a complex of several worlds of influence. For instance, we turn to a writing of Isaiah and note the factors that enter into the story, from his original experience with God to our own experience, as we read what has come to us from almost twenty-seven centuries ago. The following are major factors in the transmission:

1. Isaiah's own insights, his own capacities to see with God.

2. The language and thought world of the Jews of the day and Isaiah's facility and artistry in using this language; the writing down of his message in this language.

3. The alterations through the centuries with the copyings and "correctings" of the text.

4. The manner of selecting Isaiah's writings by those who formed the canon, whether in part or in whole.

5. The redactions by editors of his text, to make it say what they considered he was endeavoring to say.

6. The translation of the writings into languages other than the one in which he wrote with consequent adjustments.

7. The interpretation of these writings by the group in which the present reader has membership, notably the church group.

8. The ability and intent of the reader in ascertaining and appreciating what Isaiah was saying out of his communion with God.

9. The prevailing notions about what inspiration is, how God works with persons, and how these persons express themselves in inspired writing.

10. The prevailing notions about God's way of operating in his universe, of living with men. This ranges from fixed finality to ongoing fluidity.

The simpler the views on these matters, the less examination made, the more the inclination toward axiomatic approach, toward once-and-for-always interpretations. The more the person is inclined to question, the greater his likelihood to concentrate on what changes rather than on what is enduring in ongoing spirituality. Who, then, are the sound searchers for meaning and message?

Identity Rather Than Identicality

God is not in the business of producing identicals. His creative expression is always rich in variations. And this holds true for persons. When Jesus Christ selected twelve men to be his apostles he did not choose men who were all alike and he did not try to make identicals out of them. It appears that he selected twelve men who brought together a remarkable collection of outlooks, patterns, and moods. This holds throughout the Bible. <u>The Spirit of God does not take men of prophetic spirit and make them all alike. God uses the endowments of each man with expanding expression, for fruitful returns.</u>

So Isaiah spoke and wrote with the literary qualities that have been called majestic, cathedral-esque. Amos called a spade a spade and told his people to straighten up. Luke radiated his social-mindedness, his health concerns. John wrote with focus upon the fundamentals of light, life, love. Matthew wrote of Jewish genealogies. Paul looked to outreach to the Gentile world.

The discriminating interpreter catches the tone and pattern of thinking and the literary style of the scriptural writer. He sees a man in the thought world and religious setting of his times and interprets him accordingly. He does not find what is not there. He sees the man using the thought patterns, the phrasings of his day, yet sees him transcending these as the prophetic writer endeavors to see with God beyond the usual, and seeks to speak this meaningfully to his times. To be understood he has to use the language which is meaningful to his people.

In a Hebraic Setting

The Book of Mormon tells the story of three migrating groups who came out of the Near East and crossed the ocean to the Western Hemisphere. The major story speaks of a group that left Jerusalem about 600 B.C., just before the invasion of Judah by the Babylonians. <u>Their religious beliefs and practices have to be interpreted in the setting of pre-captivity Judaism.</u> Materials would be available to them that were connected in some way with the destiny of all the Jews and of this particular migrating group of Jews. There was a stretch of faith involved in leaving Jerusalem for an unknown land, departing from "the land of milk and honey" for a strange new land of promise. Would God separate them from the calling of the Jews? Would the expected Messiah know of their whereabouts and come to them?

The Jewish faith had much to say about "atonement." It provided elaborate ritualism for achieving atonement. It had much to say about using blood to effect atoning. There was the notion of eradicating a debt. The Nephite migrants spoke of "infinite atonement," as they looked to the coming of their Messiah. In current terminology, they in their distant land wanted to "be in on it."

And these Jews from the East were concerned about the role of their own people as "chosen." How could they cross the ocean, locate in a faraway land, and still be of the "chosen" ones? What was to be the relationship between the Jews, the chosen people, and the Gentiles? It was this kind of concern that prompted the early recorders to include so much about the relations of the Jews and the Gentiles. This was a very important matter to these migrants. The vision of Lehi about this was couched in symbolism meaningful to his people. The Hebrews were seen as the true olive tree. The Gentiles who would accept the Christ were identified as the outside branch who were grafted on to the true olive tree. In time the straying sprigs of the olive tree had to be brought back and grafted into the true tree.

Names, terms, rites, and doctrines were Hebraic. They have to be seen as transplanted from Jerusalem to Zarahemla.

A Prepossession with Keeping of Records

The Hebrews were "write-it-down" people. They thought of God writing down rules and regulations for them. Their God inscribed the ten commandments on a tablet of stone. Moses is credited with writing down "laws" and prescriptions for contract relations between the people and their God.

Reformers such as Josiah would get the law to the fore—
would have it read, recorded, and observed. The Law and the
Prophets were to be written and kept available. Keeping these
intact was a solemn responsibility.

The Book of Mormon discloses a kind of prepossession in
this matter. When Lehi's colony was about to leave Jerusalem, he was almost abnormally intent on procuring adequate
copies of the Jewish scripture to take along on the journey.
So earnest was the intent of this group that they went to
extreme measures to procure copies. These scriptures would
ensure continuity with their past and with their calling. The
leaders were bent on maintaining soundness in the faith of
their fathers.

And on the Western continent they were equally intent
on keeping their own records. The Book of Mormon speaks
often of a father transmitting the keeping of the people's
record to his son, with serious charge concerning the
responsibility. With such concern they would engrave their
story on the most durable materials available. Nothing would
be too precious.

Ever Were There Abridgments

Abridging was a major occupation of these ancients. In
the opening book Nephi wrote, "I do not make a full account
of the things which my father has written. . . . I make an
abridgment of the record of my father, upon plates which I
have made with my own hands" (I Nephi 1:15, 17). The
book closes with account of the abridging of the Nephite
records by Mormon and by Moroni. Moroni mentioned his
abridging of the Jaredite records (Moroni 1:1).

An abridgment reflects the interests and the choices of
the editor who redacts and abridges. There is always the
likelihood of losing the individual quality that characterized

the original writer. There is ever the possibility of reducing the several styles to the quality of the one abridging. In a sense the Book of Mormon is a "recorder's digest" with reflection of the concern of the one who edited and redacted. The remarkable thing is that so much of the original spirit and sayings of the characters has been retained.

The foreword to the Book of Mormon says, "It is an abridgment of the record of the people of Nephi and also of the Lamanites . . . and an abridgment taken from the . . . record of the people of Jared." And such a record it is. It expresses the concern of the record keepers and the abridgers—the record was to function in later centuries for the converting of the straying descendants of the first migrants to the new land. So the language is homiletic, full of warnings and appeals to repentance. It is loaded with concerns that the people of later years would do better than their forebears, who lost the intent that God had for them in the new land.

The Translator Would Use His Language Resources

Joseph Smith says he translated the record of the Book of Mormon "by the gift and power of God." He never amplified this statement. Perhaps he could not. We have to apply to his experience insights about the ministry of the Holy Spirit that come through our funds of counsel and testimony in this field. The recipient of prophetic inspiration is more than an automaton on whose inactive mental sheet God writes specific words that he transmits to sound or to writing. Sometimes this has been the notion of those who believe in what is called plenary inspiration. In this notion some would go so far as to say that even the punctuation is specifically dictated. They imply that a word used in an "authorized" version is dictated specifically by God to the scripture writer.

The counsel given to Oliver Cowdery about receiving inspired guidance and enlightenment points to the utilization of the natural and cultivated powers of the person who is being ministered to by the Good Spirit. This person senses with clarity the message to be expressed. Then he is called to express this in terms of his own thinking and speaking resources. An Isaiah would speak in the language of Isaiah; a Paul of Tarsus would think and speak in terms that are his own.

Joseph Smith would use what verbal resources he could mobilize. These would go beyond the usual manner of expression. It would be expected that the language of a farm boy of his background would condition the phrasing and organization of the story of the Book of Mormon. He would take the abridged, simple wording that he sensed made the story and then use the language skills at his command. Sentence structure and punctuation would not be his strong equipment. God would push him to the fullness of his resources and carry him beyond his ordinary form of expression.

Joseph Smith's time and environment would ever have influence in his dictating to Oliver Cowdery, his scribe. In the translating would appear the patterns of thinking and phrasing of the translator. The man who speaks for God uses the means at his disposal in the world of his thinking. These would tend to express the doctrinal forms of the time in which Joseph Smith was living. There is ever the conditioning by the resources of the prophet through whom God is working.

And this applies to the reader, too. He reads and hears through the doctrinal world that he knows. He who reads and lives the Book of Mormon will make contact with the doctrinal world of the ancient Hebrews, the migrants to the Western Hemisphere, the frontier residents of the United States in which Joseph Smith was living, and with the doctrinal world of his own day. This latter may vary from narrowness to breadth, from finality to indefiniteness. This awareness helps us interpret and use with greater insight. It also makes us aware of the complex situation God faces when he wants men to see and hear him through the scriptures of any time and place.

Scriptures Use Figures and Symbols

Jesus used parables much of the time. He wanted to go beyond the limited applications of hardheaded literalists. He wanted his teachings to be expandable and widely applicable. So he would say, "The kingdom of heaven is like . . ." He talked of sheep and their shepherd. He referred to "the lilies of the field." He likened a man to "a sower going forth to sow." He could not hem in what he had to say by the fences of contemporary words. Whenever a person of prophetic insight comes to the limits of concepts and pictures in the verbal world of his day, he launches forth in figurative language. This can be stretched and enlarged.

The Book of Mormon used figures and symbols. Humanity is pictured as one fold with one shepherd. Faith is likened to the planting of a seed with expectation of fruitage. It is spoken of as "experiment." Scriptures written in the land of the Eskimo would use different figures. In modern times writers might refer to space ships, to atomic energy, to escalators, to deep-sea diving, and more. We have to reconstruct the figurative, symbolic world of the writer of scriptures in order to catch his meaning, his message.

And Some Language Will Not Be There

Scriptures written two thousand years ago will carry the conceptions of that day. We do not look for concepts and phrases that have developed during recent decades. Modern readers do well to remember this. The writings are to be understood, not discounted because they speak a different thought language. Such a writing is evaluated in accordance with the degree that it transcends the thinking of the times and lifts insights into God beyond the coventional thinking of the day. The great prophets made this happen. Their writings are gauged in terms of their times, not in terms of the thought world of today.

Here are concepts in modern thinking we would not expect to find in the thought patterns of the Book of Mormon. These patterns of thinking were nonexistent in the times of its composition and recording.

1. *Natural law* as the descriptive statement of the predictable operation of phenomena in the universe. In those days men thought of nature operating at the command of God. The term "natural" is used frequently, but in a different meaning than we use it today. The term "law" was used then, more in the sense of a divine commandment than in the connotation of a description of operation. We have to be aware of this or we can get things confused.

2. *Process,* the flow of happenings in sequence, in relationship, so we can trace causal relationship and inter-relationship. The opposite view makes each happening an isolated event, an independent happening. Many devout believers in God think of whatever happens as brought about by an edict of God.

3. *Person and personhood.* This is a fairly new concep-tion, even if the term is of long standing. In modern conception of "person" we see personhood coming to pass in

process through interpersonal interaction. We see each coming into social relationships as a candidate to become a person. In this process the person achieves self-awareness and self-management. This continues through life.

4. *Evolution,* which signifies continuing change, ongoing development in forms, in process, with emergence of new conditions. Evolution is seen in contrast to the notion of special creation at a single time with finality in forms.

The Book of Mormon, like the Bible, speaks the language of the ancient world before such ideas as relativity, atomic energy, circulation of the blood, genetics, electricity, social organism, process and person were in man's thinking. Those who read meaningfully today have to discover the language of that ancient world of thinking and then try to speak the message in language meaningful today.

Scriptures Have Several Types of Writing

The Bible is rich in variety of writings. There are letters, sermons, poems and hymns, genealogies, history, life stories, and more. The Book of Mormon has variety, too. There are quotations from other Jewish scriptures, notably from Isaiah. There are testimonies, such as Ammon's review of what happened when he and his three brothers went as missionaries to the Lamanites (Alma 14:79 ff.). There are hymns and poems, such as Nephi's psalm, "Rejoice, O My Heart!" (II Nephi 3:30-66). There are narratives of dramatic happenings, such as Nephi's building of the ship (I Nephi 5). There are letters, such as the exchange between Captain Moroni and Governor Pahoran (see Alma 27:14 ff.). There are sermons, such as those of Jesus Christ to the Nephites and those of Alma and Amulek (Alma 7). There are patriarchal blessings such as Alma's to his three sons, Helaman, Shiblon, and Corianton (Alma 17-19). There are theological considerations, such as Nephi's dissertations to his brothers about sin and atonement (II Nephi 6 ff.). There are accounts of battles and military marches. There are sections on social collapse and sections on Zionic community life. The diversity covers quite a full range.

Readers identify the kind of writing they are perusing, and then read accordingly. A person-to-person letter or a person-to-group letter has to be read with understanding of the background of the setting and the intent of the writer. A lesson on theology, such as the writings on atonement in the books of Nephi, requires us to recover the thinking and concerns of the writer. Scripture reading requires us to live with the writer in his time. Then we must translate this into an interpretation that is meaningful today.

Pointers on Reading the Book of Mormon

1. Get inside the book, read what the original producers had to say. From these two sources designate what the book is saying it is and what it is for.

2. See the essential Hebrew background in religious thought and practices that runs through the writings of the book. Live with Jewish notions about their place and calling, about their relations with God, about the functioning of Jewish religion in everyday living, in family living.

3. Reconstruct the pictures the ancients had of the universe, the way this universe operates, and God's role in this. This picture will see and speak in terms that precede the findings of modern science.

4. Picture the book as an abridgment of longer records which condenses and summarizes, with likely diminution of the details and personal qualities of the original writers. Here is a "digest."

5. Note the unusual emphasis on keeping records and the purpose for doing so. This record-keeping was a consuming

interest. It was motivated by concern for future generations of the people on the continent. There is "preachy" intent and tone, with much pointing out of sin that led to downfall in early times.

6. Consider the motivation for including so much of Isaiah's message. A basic reason was to affirm the coming and the mission of the Messiah. These Western-land Jews were concerned about his coming, about his coming to them. Isaiah was the prophet who wrote of the Messiah and whose ministry was fairly recent yet with sufficient time lapse to afford prophetic standing.

7. Focus on the main character, Jesus Christ. It would be expected that there would be similarity, even duplication of what he taught in his Judea-Galilee ministry. There is application to the people and the setting.

Considerations for Conversation

These questions are presented to help provide focus on major considerations. They have to do with our insight into the writing and using of scriptures for the light they can contribute to our contemporary living.

1. What difference does it make in our interpretation and use of scriptures if we see God dictating the content and the words specifically or if we believe God inspires a writer through illuminating and utilizing the writer's resources?

2. How do the writings of a book in the Bible express the thinking and the writing style of a man? How do the gospel of Luke, the gospel of Matthew, and the gospel of John reveal different emphases of the same life story—different patterns of thinking, different choice of materials, different phrasings?

3. What would be the influence of editing and redacting on a record that brings together the writings of several authors? How does this operate in the formulation of the

Book of Mormon? What does this tend to do to individuality in writings?

4. A boy asked this question, "If a prophet of the time before Jesus had seen a vision of a modern airplane, how would he have pictured this to the people of his times?" How would this be interpreted by someone reading about it in modern times?

5. John spoke in the book of Revelation of "the four corners of the earth" (Revelation 7:1). How do you think a prophetic writer in our day would describe all this? What would a modern writer portray as the farthest flung section of the universe? How do you use the statement of John?

6. What elements of the ancient Hebrew religion need to be noted in the Book of Mormon and handled accordingly? Note Aaron's statement in Alma 13:13. How did the Jews consider that there had to be blood to effect atonement? How would the idea of the shedding of blood and the paying of a debt be inharmonious with the nature of God for many who are living today? What basic thing was Aaron trying to say?

7. What do you say to a person of modern times who does not see God as a king sitting on a throne? (See II Nephi 9:1-5). How was this the best portrayal available to Nephi? What portrayal of a prophet of modern times would be meaningful in the thinking of today? What happens when we insist that the phrasings of former years be held to today?

8. How do we interpret and use parables? How are they more inclusive than a single declaration in the language of the times? Lehi and Nephi visioned God's calling of the Jews and the Gentiles in terms of the olive tree and the grafting in of branches. What figure of speech would speak meaningfully to us today?

9. How does the intent of a writer condition the materials he includes in his message? What were some materials

included in the first three decades of the Reorganization that would receive less emphasis, if any at all, in today's writings? What are some topics that would be included today that would not have been included or mentioned a century ago? How does this apply to the Book of Mormon? What were concerns of some authors, some editors?

10. How might the phrase "any manner of 'ites' " (IV Nephi 1:20) be the most descriptive phrasing available to Joseph Smith in his translating in 1829? What does this mean to us now? How would you express this in the language of our times?

11. Interpret: "Scriptures speak the various languages of those who see, write, translate, and read the message." Indicate how God is conditioned in what he can say by these several languages. Enumerate the languages of those using the Book of Mormon from Nephi of ancient America to Newton Smith of modern Australia?

12. How do we need to reconstruct the story and the message of the Book of Mormon so they will be meaningful today, if we wish to use the book to guide us in our everyday living here and now?

Exploration II. The Book Speaks of God in History . . . This book is one section in the ongoing story of God's intent. What is narrated is a section in a total world program. The Jews have a specific role. History is related in the concepts of ancient thinking.

This exploration is asking, <u>What does the Book of Mormon say about God</u>? <u>How is God pictured as carrying on in history</u>? <u>What kind of God is the God of this book</u>? In these writings God will be portrayed in the thinking of the ancient world. The universe will be pretty limited in comparison with notions of the space age with its light-years. There will be nothing said about natural process and natural law. But the nature of God and the purpose of God stand forth. What does this book say that can provide guidance today?

More Than Declaring That God Is

Moderns want affirmations about God that "hold up" and "hold together." Moderns do not respond supportively to general exhortations such as "Believe in God!" and "Have faith in God!" To these exhortations they respond, "What kind of a god?" They ask for meaningful language for talking about God. They ask for portrayal of God in action, now, and over a long span of time. Moderns want more than abstractions about a God out yonder: they want descriptives of a God who is creating, working, influencing, caring here and now. The God of this book was ever doing something, ever inviting his sons to do something with him. This could be building a ship to cross the ocean or building a community of regenerated persons.

The Book Portrays the God of the Jews

The migrants from Jerusalem brought with them the highest conceptions of the God of their fathers. They used the language of Isaiah, who had lived something more than a century before their departure. Here God was righteous; he was creative; he was purposive; he was caring and loving in his attitude toward man. While the key slogan of the Jews then and today, the Shema (Deuteronomy 6:4-6), is not quoted specifically, this theme pervades the Book of Mormon.

So in the book God is concerned with man and his eternal well-being. God wants man to be his co-worker. To carry on his program for all mankind, God selects a group of people, the "sons of Abraham," to be his "chosen people." They are called in corporate national living to reveal God to the world. Then these Jews face the necessity of deciding whether they are going to consider themselves the favorites of God, "teacher's pets," with concern for advantage to themselves or if they are going to see and accept their mission to all humanity. Isaiah had focused upon this contrast. The book brings this contrast to the fore with some sharpness.

This book puts all this in a larger setting. A small group of Jews are directed to go from Jerusalem to a distant, unknown land across the mighty waters. This migration was to do more than provide escape for the colony; it was to figure in God's larger world-scene program. The scope of God's concern and operation was extended in large proportion.

In all this God is pictured in the lofty yet immediate conception of the Jews. He made a covenant with the Jews: they chose to align their way with God's. He calls men to represent him, to bring men into right relationships with him. In all this is frank awareness that men tends to get away from God, go tangent ways that alienate them from God. Then man needs atonement. He needs to get back at one with God. The Jews pictured this atoning as being done through contrition, rites that involved the shedding of blood, and renewal in righteous living. And this righteous living involved right relationships with others, as the Shema affirmed. They looked toward the coming of Messiah as the for-always Atoner who would bring men to God through the shedding of his blood. They were a long way from seeing the Messiah's atoning ministry as getting man and God together through the living and the loving of the Messiah. They were schooled in obeying rules and regulations to effect atonement. And the Messiah would want living righteousness and loving relationship.

Conceptions of God in Past, in Present

The Book of Mormon concentrates on God in action. He is portrayed in accordance with the thought patterns of those times. Those who read the book will want to get hold of the enduring basics and put them in terms meaningful today.

Then and now God can be interpreted as operating in many diverse ways: (1) As the determiner of every specific thing that happens; (2) as an absentee observer on the sidelines; (3) as an interventionist on occasions when he enters into what is going on; (4) as an operator by edict who declares, "Let this happen!"; (5) as a king on a throne who requires homage; (6) as adventurous creator; (7) as manipulator of cycles; (8) as punitive judge; (9) as consultant, when man is perplexed; and (10) as co-worker with man in father-son relationship. And there are combinations of these.

The field of God's concern is perceived in various ways. Sometimes this field is large, sometimes limited. Sometimes God is thought of as concerning himself with (1) some segment of history; (2) some chosen people; (3) some phase of life, often designated as "the spiritual"; (4) events of his liking; or (5) one side of a dualistic universe. In this latter, those who consider that the material universe is evil believe God could have nothing to do with it. There is also the inclusive view of God's concern and operation in the integrated universe.

All this involves our notions about God's place for and his estimation of man. God can be thought of (1) as making man to be his servant, his stool-pigeon; (2) as requiring man to be a yes-yes responder; (3) as expecting man to be developing in self-management to become a competent co-worker with Him. The concepts of the role of man in God's program vary from a robot condition to a "son of God" calling. A working conception of God always involves God's conception of man's place in his universe, in history.

In summary, God can be thought of as running things by decrees with each decree a thing in itself—and some make this conditional upon God's mood at the time. Some believe that if they get to God on the right side with the right appeal, he can be swayed in his deciding—and this can be seen as pretty localized. Or the universe can be seen operating in relationships, with God functioning in reliable, orderly ways that may be described in terms of natural law. Here God can be interpreted as sometimes moving out beyond the usual in accord with "natural law" we do not yet understand. This can be designated as "miracle."

A people's prevailing theory about God in history exerts definite effect upon their behavior in their patterns of living. Does God keep on the job, or does he go on recess, as Elijah told the priest of Baal he might be doing (I Kings 18:27)? Does God stay outside or does God work right in the process of things? Does God work in a corner or in all the world, in all the universe?

What is God's place in history, God's place in the universe, as pictured in the Book of Mormon? What does the book have to say that throws light on God's nature and ways?

The following are set forth in abbreviated manner as what the book says about God in history, in his universe:

1. God is the creator of all things, with intent for their wise utilization.

> "Believe in God; believe that he is, and that he created all things, both in heaven and in earth. Believe that he has all wisdom, and all power, both in heaven and in earth."—Mosiah 2:13-14.

This inclusive affirmation bothers some. They interpret this as hinting that God has created evil. Not so. God creates things and persons with manifold potential. Potential is native capacity. And this can go this direction or that direction. Evil is potential gone wrong. The inclusive process of atonement involves getting things as well as persons on the right track, in right relations. This places "all things" together in an inclusive, integrated operation.

2. God continues in creation, in communication.

> "My work is not yet finished; neither shall it be until the end of man; neither from that time henceforth and forever."—II Nephi 12:63.

Many believers in God have pictured him as starting creation at some specific time and have thought of him as "ending things" at some date. Such a view does not square with God's eternal nature. He keeps on creating forever. Whenever he discontinues creating, he will be not "I AM" but "HE WAS."

Many "scripturists" look for "the end of things" and the "end of time." There is no place for this when the book speaks for itself. With this may well go the counsel to Moses in his panoramic viewing of creation as recorded in Doctrine and Covenants 22:23:

"The heavens they are many and they can not be numbered unto man, but they are numbered unto me, for they are mine; and as one earth shall pass away, and the heavens thereof, even so shall another come; and there is no end to my works, neither to my words; for this is my work and my glory, to bring to pass the immortality, and eternal life of man."

3. God provides the earth for man's habitation and good life.

"The Lord has created the earth that it should be inhabited; and he created his children that they should possess it."—I Nephi 5:126-127.

When this statement is coordinated with other sayings of the book, we may add, "and enjoy it." The conception for many centuries was that the universe was dualistic, spiritual and material, with a discount of the material. Often there was the notion that God could not have had anything to do with creating and managing the material, for he would be contaminated by touching the unholy material. Many thought of salvation as complete deliverance from whatever is physical. The Book of Mormon states essentially what is said more succinctly in the Doctrine and Covenants later on:

"I, the Lord, stretched out the heavens, and builded the earth, as a very handy work; and all things therein are mine."—101:2d.

"All things which come of the earth, in the season thereof, are made for the benefit and the use of man, both to please the eye, and to gladden the heart; yea, for food and raiment, for taste and for smell, to strengthen the body, and to enliven the soul."—59:4d.

In the book there is no suggestion of dualism that discounts the physical. There is no suggestion of salvation through getting away from the earth. Rather is the earth to be utilized in God's way so that man can live up to his calling.

4. The way of God's universe is the way of righteousness, which is the way of happiness.

"If there be no righteousness, there be no happiness. . . . And if these things are not, there is no God."—II Nephi 1:90, 92.

The correlation of happiness and righteousness is one of the basic contributions of the Book of Mormon. The book affirms that the two go together, that peoples in history get along well when they live with the two in one program. The qualities of joy and rightness inhere in God. God intends these to have expression in the ongoing life of man.

5. The way of the universe and the way of history is contrast, antithesis.

"It must needs be, that there is an opposition in all things. . . . All things must needs be a compound in one."—II Nephi 1:81, 83.

God is portrayed as designing a universe in which there is contrast, an essential quality in the process of things. This is not the same as dualism in which one phase is to overcome the other and destroy it. Rather does this express how contrasting forces can function in opposition in a single process. Modern science has been doing some discovering about these phenomena. For instance, electricity may be thought of as motion of charged particles manifesting themselves in attraction and repulsion against other particles. The terms negative and positive are used. Modern science is also speaking of antibodies and antigens in biological phenomena. We are reminded that in healthy operation antibodies operate with sound balance.

We are thinking in social relationships how diversity, not hostility, can function in expressing life with vitality and creativity. We are seeing that sameness alone could bring deadness and deterioration. The saying in II Nephi 1:81 indicates the place for contrast which will achieve choice and creativity. Without contrast and opposition we might have an ineffective social world, with only weaklings emerging. This would hold for spiritual development, too. The conception is contrast for creativity, not animosity for annihilation.

6. God is source of goodness; evil comes out of disharmony with God.

"All things which are good come of God. . . . That which is of God invites and entices to do good continually; wherefore, everything which invites and entices to do good, and to love God, and to serve him is inspired of God."—Moroni 7:10, 11.

Moroni's comment makes an affirmation of considerable consequence. The goodness of a working God is active, dynamic, creative, not passive or static. God's kind of goodness "entices" men to line up with him in effecting this goodness. This is not a matter of refraining from what is wrong but of bringing to pass what is good, of aggressive and insistent priority of goodness over wrong. The Book of Mormon has no Zion or heaven for quiescent Saints. Goodness is to be attractive and adventurous.

7. Righteousness achieves priority in the long range of history.

"He will not suffer that the wicked destroy the righteous. He will preserve the righteous by his power. . . . Wherefore the righteous need not fear."— I Nephi 7:35-37.

This statement involves a longtime view, a moment in a stream of ongoing living. The Book of Mormon looks at God's planning through the centuries. For instance, the Jews may be out of step and off the course for a time, but eventually they will come into line. The story of the Nephites and the Lamanites seems to close with a victory for the wrong. The writers insist that the Nephites had deteriorated and could not be considered as "righteous." In the years ahead the Lamanites would hear and respond. There are no half-minute realizations of righteousness in the book.

When Joseph Smith was translating the Book of Mormon he ran into a frustrating experience. Some of the manuscript had been lost and he had lost the ability to translate. This counsel came to him: "The works and the designs, and the purposes of God cannot be frustrated." There might be delay and obstruction but not defeat. The book reminds us to get the longtime and the large-scale perspective. It reminds us that God does not operate in split-second hurry-ups. And it affirms that in the long range of history righteousness comes out on top.

8. God designated a chosen people for the accomplishment of his purpose.

> "He loved our fathers; and he covenanted with them, even Abraham, Isaac, and Jacob; and he remembered the covenants which he had made."—I Nephi 5:132.

Concern about the role of the Jews as "chosen people" pervades the book. When Lehi and his family left Jerusalem, the fall of that city to the Babylonians was imminent and captivity was in sight. What was to be the future of the Jews? When this company took leave for a distant hemisphere, would they still be chosen Jews? Would Messiah come to them, too? Then when the Nephites declined in spirituality and dropped to extinction, what was to happen to the Lamanites? Would they be dropped from their calling? The book sees all this in terms of the centuries. It sees "chosenness" in terms of fitness and function for this calling.

9. God uses the Gentiles for his purpose as the Jews fall short.

> "After our seed are scattered, the Lord God will proceed to do a marvelous work among the Gentiles, which shall be of great worth to our seed.... And it shall also be of worth to the Gentiles."—I Nephi 7:17, 19.

The foreword of the book is addressed "to Jew and Gentile." The eventuality that is visioned is that of a world fraternity in which both Jew and Gentile are united in loyalty to Jesus Christ. The figure of speech of the olive tree images a time when the tree consists of the main Jewish stock, the Gentile branches grafted in, and the erstwhile recalcitrant Jews re-grafted to the main tree. In this situation there is no priority or favoritism for either Jew or Gentile.

10. God designs the Western land to be a land of promise, a place of liberty in his longtime program, opening it to Gentiles as expedient for his total work.

> "A land which is choice above all other lands, ... a land of liberty.... To the righteous, it shall be blessed forever.... It is wisdom that this land should be kept as yet from the knowledge of other nations."—II Nephi 1:6 ff.

This carries the tone of what Paul of Tarsus said in Athens, "[God] hath made of one blood all nations of men for to dwell on all the face of the earth, and hath determined the times before appointed, and the bounds of their habitation" (Acts 17:26). On first thought this sounds like a schedule with definitized happenings. On second thought it speaks of God's worldwide and centuries-long program of carrying on what he has in mind to achieve: an inclusive family of mankind. It responds to the once common inquiry, "Did God know anything about the Western Hemisphere and the Indians before Columbus told him about them?" Sometimes the bungling responses of men interfered with the achievement of what God had in mind.

11. Zion emerges as core community in God's purpose and program.

"Blessed are they who shall seek to bring forth my Zion at that day, for they shall have the gift and the power of the Holy Ghost."—I Nephi 3:187.

"What shall one then answer the messengers of the nations? 'That the Lord hath founded Zion, and the poor of his people shall trust in it.' "—II Nephi 10:54.

Here Zion is not some afterthought, some community with privilege for the chosen, favored ones. It is more than a Jewish city clustered around the temple on Mount Moriah. Here a people live together with corporate expression of God's way of life, with a mission in ministering to the world. This Zion is a community of alert, active sons and daughters of God who vigilantly keep the Zionic way of living flourishing (note the warnings in II Nephi 12:20, 25). Such a community is seen as a spiritual nucleus in the great wide worldly world.

12. The life and ministry of the Messiah is central in human history.

"Jesus is the Christ, the Eternal God, manifesting himself unto all nations" (from prefatory statement in book, page iii).

This word "manifesting" carries significant meaning. One youth defined the word well: "appearing so that whatever it is, is clearly seen." The book has Jesus Christ visit the

Western land so that he is "clearly seen." This is more than looking at the figure of Christ; this means spiritual perception, too. Those who would see the Christ would see what God is.

The Book of Mormon makes the coming of Christ Jesus, the Son of God, the key happening in human history, the core happening in the book.

The Book Affirms Purpose in History

The Book of Mormon never hints that everything in history turns out in a just-right way. There is no heralding of the message, "God's in his heaven—all's right with the world!" The book says that many things are not right, that many things do not turn out as God intends. The human factor is seen as ever so important and influential. But the message of the book is not one of despondency and doom. There is the call to see and to plan for "the long run"—but never for the "long wait." Man is to get with God and make the right things happen.

the doctrine of the last / final things death resurrection immortality judgment The viewpoint of Book of Mormon eschatology is simple: "History is going somewhere, it will keep going, and it will bring God's way through!" The span of time will seem short to moderns who think in terms of light-years, but it was ever so stretched to those of those ancient times. The book affirms that in spite of frustrating hostilities and the indifference of man, God's way is forging ahead into realization.

The book speaks out against notions of nihilists and materialists. It breaks with the view of Bertrand Russell that "man is the product of causes which have no prevision of the end they are achieving." The story of life is more than Hamlet saw it, "a tale told by an idiot, full of sound and fury, signifying nothing." Yes, what takes place is conditioned by man who is a determiner of his destiny, but he is not the only factor in determination. God is in the story, too.

The directives that come out of Book of Mormon eschatology are simple, but sound and servicing. (1) See events in inclusive framework, God's framework. (2) Live together in the world with hope and high expectancy. (3) Make right things happen with sense of responsibility, that these will fit into and contribute to the longtime flow of life. (4) Search to discover from God the direction to take, the goals to achieve. Then will come happiness, realized through righteousness. And believers will identify what constitutes happiness and righteousness.

Toward a Theology of History

Only recently has there been much concern with working out a theology of history. It was usually presumed that God makes things happen by edicts, that whatever happens is on God's schedule. Often men have bowed to whatever was taking place as if God wanted things to go that way. The meek would submit and say, "Thy will be done." Sometimes believers have studied the Bible to try to discover God's schedule, often hunting passages and "prophecies" here and there to substantiate a schedule they have worked out.

More recently moderns have been looking at happenings in history and saying something like this: "Things do not make any sense. If God manages things this way, he is a pretty poor manager." And some ask, "Does history make sense, or is it a running story of meaningless happenings?"

The Book of Mormon is a story of an endeavor that did not work out all the time as God would have had it. There were times of spiritual heights and there were times of human degradation. The Book of Mormon brings in the human factor very forcefully. It affirms the postulate of modern science that all things exist in relationships. It makes this inclusive; it says that God and God's universe have to be included in these relationships. It says that all humanity has to be included in these relationships. The Book of Mormon does not say that everything that happens is of God's designing. It calls men to catch hold of what God's design is for making history turn out his way.

Considerations for Conversation

1. How can the Book of Mormon be used to extend the scope of God in history? How can it be interpreted and used to narrow the picture of God's operations?

2. Is the theology of history in the Book of Mormon materialistic, dualistic, or ? Materialism holds that the controlling factors in history are materialistic, economic. Dualism places matter in opposition to the spiritual. Christian Science denies the existence of the material. What is the interpretation of the Book of Mormon?

3. Arnold Toynbee has formulated a philosophy of history in which he asserts the need to see the wholeness of things. He affirms that civilizations have gone down as they have lost their vitality and creative power from within. He sets forth that in a healthy civilization there are minorities of creative and consecrated spirit who contribute to the good of the whole and that when these decline the civilization goes down. What is the thinking of the Book of Mormon in this field?

4. How does the Book of Mormon say the "chosen people" lost their "chosenness"? How did the Nephites forfeit their calling, their right to continuance? What were they expected to do in God's longtime program?

5. Does the Book of Mormon picture God as observer, interventionist, judge, king on a throne, absentee landlord, or what?

6. What does the Book of Mormon suggest would happen to man and to human life if God were to impose a situation

without contrast, without "opposition," with "innocence" in man? Does opposition mean fight between good and evil, or what? What are explorations in physical and biological sciences finding out about "opposition"? Do you see God providing for opposition in spiritual phenomena?

7. How is it so necessary that we indicate what happiness and righteousness mean when we say the two are inseparable? How might we identify them so they would be either hostile to or inadequate in God's program for man in his universe?

8. How do you see the discovery and settlement of America well timed in history for the achieving of the mission of the Western land? What if this discovery and settlement had taken place about A.D. 1100? What contributions did Gentiles bring to America that provided foundation for what God had in mind?

9. Does the Book of Mormon suggest that human history will come to an end at some appointed time with a heavenly suprahuman history then taking place? Is there an end of time, an end of things in our eschatology?

10. Do you see the Book of Mormon picturing God concerned with "life after death" or with "life before death" or with "two in one" in a total program? Does the book stress living elsewhere or living here on earth?

11. How does the Book of Mormon picture a "chosen people," a Zion, a church as instrumentation to be developed for achieving God's total program through history?   p.40

Exploration III. The Book Speaks of Man's Nature and Relationships . . . In this book's thinking <u>man is designed for living with God</u>. Often man gets out of line with God and with his fellows. Then discord results. Onetime goodness can collapse.

Today religious inquirers are asking whether theology should start with God or with man. There has been a growing feeling that religious thinking has tended to put God far away and man far down. Now we are sensing that the two are not to be separated. <u>One does not understand God without understanding what God has in mind for man, and one does not understand man without seeing him in contextual relationship with God.</u> So we look into the Book of Mormon to discover what it has to say about man's nature and man's relationships. This includes man's relationship with God, with God's universe, with God's other men.

A Major Question in Religion Today

The psalm writer asked a long time ago a question that we have been asking and are still asking today. He asked it of God: "<u>What is man that thou shouldst be mindful of him, and the son of man that thou shouldst care for him?</u>" (Psalm 8:4). Through the centuries answers have been formulated. Many of these are called into question. Now it is recognized that one of the urgent needs in religion is a sound, functional, inclusive conception of what man is, of what man can become. At the World Council of Churches meeting in Upsala, Sweden, in the summer of 1968 a committee was appointed to work for three years to formulate such a concept and then bring back their report. The committee was to utilize what was available in scriptures and in science. If the church is to speak effectively to moderns it must have a meaningful theology of man.

Away from Ideas of Depravity

One youth was asked what religion has to say about man. His answer, "Man is down in the dumps and can't get himself out." Traditional theology has had much to say of man's "fall." With this came loss of ability to will anything good. Then man suffered from depravity. His physical body was evil and his biological drives were carnal. Many consigned all men to hell and arranged for some to be saved that they might glorify God. This view was caught up in the hymn that sang of Jesus Christ's coming to earth to save "such a worm as I."

Quite recently there has been a trend to the other extreme. Man has come to be thought of as "the god" who manages his own affairs. In all this "God" is discounted, dethroned, and discarded. To the fore come such words as "autonomy." Moderns sing "Invictus" with W. E. Henley, "I am the master of my fate, I am the captain of my soul." God does not matter anymore: God is dead!

Modern studies of man go into several fields of science, to anthropology, to biology, to psychology, to sociology, and more. These bring in data from biochemistry to genetics. Much of the time the total man is not seen; he is segmentalized, compartmentalized. Nor is the total universe seen, the universe in which man lives. Generally spiritual reality is left out.

The call today is to see the total man in his total environment, in total relationship with God, God's universe, and God's men. Does the Book of Mormon have anything to contribute? Is man depraved, incapable of willing anything good? Is man a two-part creature with the physical and the spiritual opposed to each other? Is man living here in a probationary state with the real life coming in the hereafter? What was the role of Jesus Christ in all this? Let the Book of Mormon speak for itself.

1. *All men are included in God's creation, in God's concern.*

"Know ye not that I, the Lord your God, created all men, and that I remember those who are upon the isles of the sea...? And I bring forth my word to the children of men, even upon all the nations of the earth?"—II Nephi 12:56, 57.

This quotation has to be interpreted in light of the inclusive message of the book. Some religionists believe that God created all men, but that he did not create them equal. The book has no castes, no priorities in this creating: all men are intended to constitute one fraternity. And God created the whole man. Some notions of yesteryear connected God only with the spiritual, for it was believed that God would have been contaminated had he had anything to do with material men.

2. *Man was created in the image of God, for eternal living.*

"Behold, I am Jesus Christ. ... In me shall all

mankind have life, and that eternally, even they who shall believe on my name; and they shall become my sons and my daughters. . . . Seest thou that ye are created after my own image? Even all men were created in the beginning after my own image."—Ether 1:77-80.

"A prophet of the Lord . . . said to them that Christ . . . should take upon him the image of man, and it should be the image after which man was created in the beginning; . . . he said that man was created after the image of God, and that God should come down among the children of men, and take upon him flesh and blood, and go forth upon the face of the earth."—Mosiah 5:43-45.

Rightly we ask, What is the image of God? Some insist on the biological likeness. Today some inquiring persons are wondering whether people on other planets will have the same exterior appearance and biological functioning as we have on the earth. They are saying that these who make God look like us humans on the earth are restricting God and personhood. These insist that the realness of God is not to be confined to physical appearance.

The Book of Mormon does not hold to this biological imagery. Rather it stresses the imagery as a person. Our modern explorations are bringing to the fore that the essence of being a person is in self-management, in self-evaluation, in self-awareness. This should keep developing and remain vital throughout the total span of life. The essence of personhood is something that cannot be weighed in physical scales or measured by a physical ruler. Nor is this something that can be stored in a museum or a refrigerator. Personhood is ever functioning. Personhood exists in relationships. The truly developing person functions with ever advancing, ever enlarging relationship with God. So one would ask, How do I love like God? How do I think like God? How do I plan like God? How do I create like God? How do I relate like God? The living of man is intended to achieve eternal quality.

3. *Man is endowed with potential for choosing, for being responsible.*

"Therefore, cheer up your hearts, and remember that you are free to act for yourselves."—II Nephi 7:40.

"Wherefore, the Lord God gave to man that he should act for himself."—II Nephi 1:99.

"Behold, you are free; you are permitted to act for yourselves; for God has given to you a knowledge, and he has made you free."—Helaman 5:85.

Man's stewardship is to discover potentials for choosing, to develop them, and to keep them in functioning condition. The Book of Mormon pictures the men of God as square-shouldered, straightforward persons who use their thinking apparatus and accord with God in their thinking.

The book pictures those who warp their thinking. Man's powers can be warped by prejudices, by phobias, by self-centeredness. They can be made subject to misdirected wants and drives. They can be enslaved today by drugs and liquors; man can become so addicted and enslaved that he is no longer able to choose. And some can deny man's stewardship in choosing and dump responsibility on God in a "leave it with him" stance. The book reveals that choosing with God calls for breadth, intent, exercise.

Foremost in this affirmation of the assignment of man to choose is the instruction given to the Saints in August

1831, when they were beginning a Zionic community in Jackson County. These pioneers were to lead out with initiative, in creative expression, in well designed planning.

"Men should be anxiously engaged in a good cause, and do many things of their own free will, and bring to pass much righteousness; for the power is in them, wherein they are agents unto themselves. . . . He that doeth not anything until he is commanded, and receiveth a commandment with doubtful heart, and keepeth it with slothfulness, the same is damned."—Doctrine and Covenants 58:6d, f.

This is the viewpoint expressed in the book.

4. _Righteousness and happiness go together in God's design for man._

"If there be no righteousness, there be no happiness."—II Nephi 1:90.

"Men are, that they might have joy."—II Nephi 1:115.

"Wickedness never was happiness."—Alma 19:74.

"It came to pass that we lived after the manner of happiness."—II Nephi 4:43.

The Book of Mormon is powerful in its affirmation that God designs that man is to be happy with eternal quality of happiness. This is more than ephemeral gaiety that slushes on the surface. The happiness pictured calls for capacity in persons, in society, for happiness in depth. Such capacity involves sensitivity and store of experience for both joy and sorrow. The truly great person has the capacity to suffer and to rejoice. There is need to identify what enduring happiness is. There is need to ascertain how man is going to achieve this happiness. Certainly the Book of Mormon does not suggest that each of us should be a gloomy Gus or a griping George. Saints are not pictured as weeping and weary and wan. God's men are joyously creative, happily fraternal, confidently cheerful.

5. *Man develops through effective choice-making.*

"Be faithful to his words, and choose eternal life, according to the will of his Holy Spirit."—II Nephi 1:123.

"To bring about his eternal purposes in the end of man, . . . there must be an opposition. . . . The Lord God gave to man that he should act for himself."—II Nephi 1:97, 99.

"If [men had not chosen] they would have remained in a state of innocence, having no joy, for they knew no misery, doing no good."—II Nephi 1:111-113.

The Book of Mormon never pictures spoon-fed Saints, eating celestial pabulum. Man is to develop in choice-making in the laboratory of living. Spiritual endowment equips man for choosing. Saintly conduct is not a matter of automatic goodness but of chosen conduct. And men are to live together under conditions that are conducive to good choosing in resources, in atmosphere, in cooperation, in guidance from God.

6. *True saintly living brings joy and satisfaction in doing good.*

"They should impart of their substance of their own free will and good desires toward God."—Mosiah 9:62.

"Charity is the pure love of Christ, and it endures forever; . . . pray to the Father with all the energy of heart, that you may be filled with this love . . . that you may become the sons of God."—Moroni 7:52, 53.

"I would desire that you should consider the blessed and happy state of those that keep the commandments of God."—Mosiah 1:88.

Wholesome religion teaches satisfaction in living right with God. There is joy "in doing good." In healthy living what we do and what we want to do accord. There are no civil wars inside persons in which duty and desire clash. There is no place for the testimony, "I do not want to do it, but God tells me to." Rather is there place for surveying our working with God and saying, "It is good." Motivation does not come of fear or desire for reward but of intent to lift, to leaven some life, and to move society in God's direction. This high quality of joy and satisfaction is expressed in Ammon's review of what had taken place when he and his three brothers went to the Lamanites as missionaries. He could say with rejoicing, "We have been made instruments in the hands of God to bring about this great work" (Alma 14:82).

7. *The natural way is the way of lining up with God, of loving with God.*

The meaning of the word "natural" is bothersome to many readers of the Book of Mormon. It has to be seen in the total context, with realization that there are two connotations to the word. In the topic sentence here the word "natural" conveys the contemporary meaning. We have to find out what the word meant in the Book of Mormon. In many places in the Book of Mormon "natural" implies apartness from God. In Mosiah 1:119 we find this sentence, "The natural man is an enemy to God." Here it is said that man is to "yield to the enticings of the Holy Spirit, and put off the natural man, and become a saint." In Alma 19:75 the "state of nature" is identified with a "carnal state" and with being in "the bonds of iniquity." This would seem to suggest that man is truly depraved and that his drives are iniquitous. It is imperative that this be read in this meaning of "natural"—that is, with the notion of man's being apart from God.

There is also the implication that the "natural" state of man is the condition in which man is aligned with God, as God designs him to be naturally. The unnatural condition exists when man gets away from God. It is said that Christ came to man on earth in order to restore this natural state. The atoning of Christ is to bring man again to this natural relationship with God, his Father. Christ effects a reconciling relationship that restores oneness between man and God (Jacob 3:16). The relation of father and son is the original or natural relationship between man and God. Alma put the matter this way: "It is requisite that all things should be restored to their proper order" (Alma 19:64). This restoration brings to pass the "natural way."

It is high time that moderns see the living in right relations with God, in communion with God, in co-working with God as the natural way.

8. *The wholeness of man's personhood and resources are involved in good living.*

"If thine eye be single, thy whole body shall be full of light."—III Nephi 5:113.

"The words which I had often heard my father speak, concerning eternal life, and the joy of the saints had sunk deep into my heart.... There came a voice to me, saying,... thy sins are forgiven thee.... Thy faith hath made thee whole."—Enos 1:4, 7, 11.

Jesus talked of wholeness in the Western lands as he had done in Eastern lands. He told his disciples that there was no such thing as hyphenated spirituality. He told his people in Land Bountiful that if the eye was single—that is, directed to one great loyalty in God—the "whole body shall be full of light" (III Nephi 5:113). He referred to healthiness as wholeness (III Nephi 8:10). This involved every segment of body and spirit. Moroni closed his writing with admonition that all who "come to Christ" would come and love him with all their "might, mind, and strength." The entire book envisions a person as a unity, with wholeness effected through a harmonizing, enlivening loyalty to Jesus Christ.

Moroni contrasts healthiness and sickness and comments that "little children are whole" (8:9). Today we are seeing that young children tend to express the natural qualities of curiosity, of spontaneity, of hopefulness, of personal integration until they get into social surroundings that stifle some things, that bring conflict and division within the child. Jesus centered on little children when he met with the Nephites at Bountiful. They were whole.

9. *Understanding love, creative love, characterizes the man of God.*

"Press forward with a steadfastness in Christ, having a perfect brightness of hope, and a love of God and of all men."—II Nephi 13:29.

"He commanded them that there should be no contention one with another, but that they should look forward with one eye, having one faith and one baptism, having their hearts knit together in unity and in love, one toward another."—Mosiah 9:54.

The Book of Mormon never depicts love as gushy good feeling. Man has to learn how to love, how to be loved. Man truly must learn what God's love is if he is to love effectively, enduringly. King Benjamin told his people that they should "be filled with the love of God" (Mosiah 2:22). Love for another meant providing him with the necessities for living, when such necessities were needed. And this giving was to be done "in wisdom and order" (Mosiah 2:44). This reaching out to another included "relief, both spiritually and temporally, according to their wants" (Mosiah 2:43). All this visions what is to the best interest of the recipient of the gifts.

This kind of love presumes a healthy consideration and evaluation of one's own self. There is no discounting of the one who loves, of the one who is loved. Alma taught his people "that every man should love his neighbor as himself" (Mosiah 11:16). The disciple does not degrade or discount himself. Jesus kept telling his own men that their love for others was to be the kind of love they had for themselves. Many moderns cannot have love for others because they do not have any love for themselves. The circle of love includes God, every man, and ourselves. The Book of Mormon teaches us to stand straight and tall as sons of God and in love help all others to stand straight and tall in relation to God who is ever straight and tall. The book directs us away from concern about being loved. It points to loving others and implies making ourselves lovable. It suggests what Eric Fromm calls developing "the capacity to love." The Saint who truly loves has to expand, refine, and direct his whole personhood so he has capacity for enduring and enlivening love for all people. At the center is the love for God and the love from God.

A Man of the Book Who Stood Tall

The Book of Mormon begins with an account of the life of Nephi of Jerusalem and of the family of his father Lehi. The story opens in true Eastern fashion with the pronoun and name, "I, Nephi." This was common in the Near East. Inscriptions on monuments erected by kings usually began this way. The picture of Nephi is that of a man in the vigor of his powers who moved out adventurously with God. He wrote of himself that he was "a man large in stature" and that he had "received much strength of the Lord" (I Nephi 1:135). He also wrote that he was "exceedingly young" when the story opened, but "large in stature" (I Nephi 1:47). This young man, often taken as a model in the book, seemed always to be moving out on some new project, always required to use his initiative. There was no notion of opening his hands so the Lord would fill them without effort on his part. His life was a blending of believing and building. This conception of the way God would work with him is caught up in his youthful affirmation to his father.

"I will go and do the things which the Lord has commanded, for I know that the Lord gives no commandments to the children of men save he shall prepare a way for them that they may accomplish the thing which he commands them."—I Nephi 1:65.

This faith was not the namby-pamby variety; it was courageous, active trust in God that saw God and Nephi working together. When God looked forward to the emergence of Zion there was no dream of a ready-made city descending for easy occupation by the Saints. The Saints were to work with God in building it. Just so God declared, "Blessed are they who shall seek to bring forth my Zion. . . . They shall have the gift and power of the Holy Ghost."

This picture of God and of man pervades the book.

A Man Who Adventured Courageously

What kind of men are the heroes of the book? One of these was Ammon, one of the four sons of King Mosiah.

He had been caught up in the negativism and the cynicism of his friend Alma. This Alma was a dynamic fellow with ability to draw others with him (Mosiah 11:159 ff.). When Alma was converted, he drew these sons of Mosiah with him. They wanted to do "a new thing." They renounced their succession to the throne of their father and set out on a fourteen-year mission to the Lamanites (Mosiah 12). They left Zarahemla and launched forth into the wilderness, providing their own food on the way. Ammon and his brothers were not going on some pink-tea venture. They were going "to a wild, and a hardened, and a ferocious people, a people who delighted in murdering the Nephites, and robbing, and plundering them." These men risked their lives with complete daring. They went with conviction that their God was a risking God, too, and would be with them on their venture. They went with thrilling expectation. When Ammon reviewed the happenings of these fourteen years, he could say, "My heart is brimming with joy!" (Alma 14:91) His joy came out of his realization of what had been taking place among the Lamanites. Now they were brothers. Ammon and his brothers had undertaken their missionary journey against the advice and amid the taunts of their own people (Alma 14:105). Many of the Nephites considered it wiser to wage war with the Lamanites than to have faith in them.

Ammon stands out as a hero of the book. He was practical and concerned with practical matters. He was a laboring man, a sheepherder for the Lamanite king Lamoni. He rose above social fences and spiritual barriers. He cared for persons. He worked with God. As one youth said, "He got a whale of a kick" out of his missionary outreach to others. He was God's type of man.

Considerations for Conversation

1. How and why is consideration of the nature of man considered so important in modern religious thinking? How have traditional doctrines been proving inadequate?

2. Identify segmented, partial ideas about what man is. What do these partial views tend to leave out of man's whole nature?

3. Asceticism is the longtime view that man has two parts, the physical and the spiritual, and that they are in opposition to each other. In this view man is to deny and depress the physical in order that the spiritual may grow. Do you find any traces of asceticism in the Book of Mormon?

4. How do some interpret sayings about "natural man" in the Book of Mormon to imply that man's original nature is evil? What does such a view do to the picture of God, to the picture of man? What is this "natural man" in the Book of Mormon that is considered evil?

5. What kind of person is held up as spiritually heroic in the Book of Mormon? What qualities are set to the fore in these heroes?

6. What is the conception of happiness that is set forth in the Book of Mormon as the happiness that man is to experience as he lives with God?

7. What does the Book of Mormon depict as the kind of joy and satisfaction that a person can experience as he gets busy with God, doing God's work?

8. How does the Book of Mormon stress abundant living here and now on this earth?

9. What kind of person do you see God having in mind as he sets out to develop persons through their working with him?

10. What can the Book of Mormon contribute to the modern-life questions, "Who am I?" and "What am I here for?" and "Where am I going?"

11. What are some conditions, some factors pointed out in the Book of Mormon that will reduce man's competency in personhood? What are some factors in modern life that do this?

12. Samuel the Lamanite said to the Nephites, "You are permitted to act for yourselves; God has made you free" (Helaman 5:85). What is this freedom? How do we achieve it? What do we do with it? How do we maintain it and enlarge it?

Exploration IV. The Book Centers on the Universal Christ . . . The first writings look forward to the coming of Christ. This Christ is interpreted in terms of Hebrew ideas concerning atonement. The high point of the book is the advent of Christ to the peoples of the Book of Mormon.

In the Book's Foreword

In a prefatory page (iii) of the Book of Mormon is a statement that speaks succinctly the mission and the message of this collection of writings. It is simple and clear. It sets forth as the purpose and theme of the book to affirm "that Jesus is the Christ, the Eternal God, manifesting himself to all nations." This statement, printed on a page by itself and placed at the forepart of the book, might prove advantageous. Everything else in the collection of writings centers around and upon this basic. Here is presented the ever living, the all-loving Christ. This universal Christ is to be revealed to all persons, to all peoples.

The verb is a present-tense, active expression. It denotes continuing revelation of this Christ. He is to be *manifesting* himself *always* and to all. He is alive. In the Book of Mormon Jesus Christ is more than a memory, more than a used-to-be figure, more than a name to be used for social control. He is more than material for liturgy, a tenet in doctrine, a concept about atonement and salvation. In the Book of Mormon Jesus Christ is a person, who comes to the Western continent to live in personal relations with humans on earth. He wanted his people to see who he was and is. He wanted them to see through him who and what God really is.

Of Full Divinity

The Book of Mormon never presents Jesus Christ as a second-rate God. Many Christians refer to "God" as supreme and then talk of Christ as if he were of lower estate. There is nothing of this in the Book of Mormon. The foreword designates Christ as "Eternal God."

One day a man with a hostile attitude toward the Book of Mormon burst out at his neighbor, "Why aren't you people Christians instead of Mormons?" The neighbor waited a moment to get his bearings. At once the indignant man said, "I mean just that. Our Bible talks of Jesus Christ. Your Mormon Bible talks about Joseph Smith." By this time the neighbor had caught the point of view of his pseudo inquirer and was ready to make reply. He spoke quietly, assuredly. "The Book of Mormon does not mention Joseph Smith. The main character in it is Jesus Christ. Everything else points to him and from him. The Book of Mormon says that Jesus Christ visited the Western continent and ministered after he had finished his work in Judah and Galilee. Let me read you something from the book." What do you suppose he read? What passage would he select to read to his complaining friend? What would you choose to read?

What the Book Affirms About Jesus Christ

The major group of Jews spoken of in the Book of Mormon left Jerusalem about 600 B.C. They got away just before the invasion of Judah by the Babylonians. They brought the scriptures of the Jews. They clung especially to the manuscripts of Isaiah. His writings spoke of the coming of Messiah in beautiful, glowing language. These migrating Jews were very concerned that they would not be left out, that Messiah would come to them. This explains why Nephi included so much of Isaiah in his copy. The Messianic hope was engrained in the Nephites. Later teachers and prophets talked of the Christ.

When Abinadi stood before King Noah and his courtiers, he declared his faith unflinchingly. He turned on the shallow, self-centered priests and denounced them. He pointed out all mankind's need for forgiveness. He spoke the familiar words of Isaiah, "All we like sheep have gone astray." Men were needing a shepherd who would live among them and call them back to the fold. In this context he spoke of the coming of Jesus Christ. This was his affirmation.

"I would that you should understand that God himself shall come down among the children of men and shall redeem his people. Because he dwells in flesh, he shall be called the Son of God. . . . The Father and Son—they are one God, the very eternal Father of heaven and of earth."—Mosiah 8:28-31.

Abinadi turned on these priests of Noah for neglect of duty and for their misrepresentation of God. He told them that if they had been teaching the law of Moses rightly, they would be looking for the Messiah to come and live among them. This was his charge to them: "Teach them that redemption comes through Christ the Lord, who is the very eternal Father" (Mosiah 8:91).

Then Noah and his priests confronted Abinadi with the charge of sacrilege. In such cases it is more appealing to charge an accused person with heresy than to admit heinous crimes in one's own living. So Noah made this accusation, "You have said that God himself should come down among the children of men" (Mosiah 9:11). The insincerity of the accusers is shown in their claim that Abinadi should be put to death for his heresy about God while saying that he would be released if he would recall his charges against them. Abinadi did not recant. He died a martyr. Noah and his priests never caught what Abinadi was affirming about this Christ.

The Premonitory Warning of Samuel

A few years before the birth of Jesus Christ, Samuel, a Lamanite, came to the Nephites in the city of Zarahemla (Helaman 5). He preached that at Christ's coming there should be attendant signs in the sky and on earth (Helaman 5:55 ff.). One special sign promised was that "a new star" should arise. Samuel said that at a later time there should be signs, more sombre and destructive, attending Christ's death (5:75 ff.). The hostile Zarahemlites were not inclined to receive Samuel's message. He had to flee from the country.

The doubters and the disbelievers got together in dialogue. They concluded that "it is not reasonable that such a being as a Christ shall come." Yet they asked, "Will he not show himself in this land as well as in the land of Jerusalem?" (Helaman 5:131). Many concluded that the whole story was a traditional myth that ignorant persons might believe. Now there came to be a dividing time: some believed and repented; others scoffed and made life miserable for believers.

The Signs Were Manifest

The star appeared. There were days of light, when at the going down of the sun, there was no darkness. After a lapse of years came darkness, storms, earthquakes with ever so much distress (III Nephi 4:6 ff.). Repentant believers concluded that Christ had been put to death.

They wondered what was going to take place after all

these sobering signs and wonders. Would the Messiah come to them?

The Advent of Christ

The fifth chapter of III Nephi is a key section of the Book of Mormon. This is the part of the book that many consider the beginner should read first. It tells of the advent of Jesus Christ. The salutation announcing him has a familiar wording. It is the salutation that was heard at the baptism of Jesus (Matthew 3:46) and at his transfiguration (Matthew 17:4). It is the salutation addressed to Joseph Smith in Palmyra Grove: "This is my beloved Son: hear him!"

Here let the book speak for itself. There is a dignified simplicity in the account. There were no spectacular displays for cowing the people. The voice was penetrating, understandable. The people came to Jesus and met him. He talked with them as a friend would converse with friends. There was more than a mass assembly: Jesus recognized persons. He called Nephi out of the congregation and blessed him (III Nephi 5:18-21). He "called others" (5:22). His school of disciples began right there and then. He pictured what the life of a saint should be. He told them that all things "had become new" (III Nephi 7:3).

Read the Advent as Told by Nephi!

Here is a time and place to let the book tell its own story. The following is an abridged version of what Nephi said. Every person, every group, every congregation should read this abridged account aloud; read it together and let it come alive today.

"It came to pass that there were a great multitude gathered together, of the people of Nephi, round about the temple which was in the land Bountiful . . . and they were conversing about this Jesus Christ, of whom the sign had been given concerning his death. . . . While they were thus conversing one with another, they heard a voice as if it came out of heaven. . . . It was not a harsh voice, neither was it a loud voice; nevertheless . . . it pierced them that heard to the center. . . .

"The third time they heard the voice and opened their ears to hear it. . . . And it said to them, 'Behold, my beloved Son, in whom I am well pleased, in whom I have glorified my name. Hear ye him!' As they understood, they cast their eyes up again toward heaven; and, behold, they saw a man descending out of heaven . . . and he came down and stood in the midst of them; and the eyes of the whole multitude were turned upon him. . . . He stretched forth his hand and spoke to the people, saying, 'Behold, I am Jesus Christ. . . . I am the light and the life of the world.' "

Christ Called Ministers

Nephi was among the people when Jesus Christ summoned him to come to him. Then Jesus "called others." There was no priority of position, no elevation in office involved in the calling. The Master said pointedly, "Ye are they whom I have chosen to minister unto this people" (III Nephi 6:2). His first instructions were not about usages or quorums or rites: he conversed with them about Christian living. He made spiritual integrity basic. He started at once a laboratory school, an on-the-job training program for these men he was calling. These twelve men (see III Nephi 9:4) began their teaching at once. The assembly was so large it was divided into twelve groups with each man a teaching, pastoral minister (III Nephi 9:6).

The calling and ordaining of men continued. As some grew older, as some died, "there were other disciples ordained in their stead" (IV Nephi 1:16). The ministering was to continue.

The Other Sheep

One of the noteworthy messages of Jesus Christ in the land Bountiful was his testimonial interpretation of "the other sheep." In Judea Jesus had referred to himself as "the good shepherd." He had spoken of the relations between him and his sheep, making this a person-with-person relationship in which the shepherd calls "his own sheep by name" (John 10:4). Once he told how the shepherd would leave "the ninety and nine" and go out to search for the one lost sheep. He intended that every sheep should have "abundant life" (John 10:10). Then he added, "Other sheep I have, which are not of this fold." He would bring all these together with "one fold and one shepherd" (John 10:16).

Jesus Christ told the people of the Western continent that he was referring to them when he spoke of his "other sheep." He added that the narrowness of the Jews did not permit them to grasp what he had in mind. Then he went on to say that there were many more sheep to whom he should be going. Again he affirmed that there should be "one fold and one shepherd."

Here is universal spiritual fellowship in full inclusiveness. No person or people would be excluded. Jesus Christ did not indicate that there would be separate pens for different sheep. There was to be one fold. Nor did he ever hint that there would be special corners for the high-status sheep and other corners for the scrub sheep. There would be difference, but there would be oneness. With such a view he said, "I am going to my other sheep."

This is another treasured portion of the book that should speak for itself. It should be read in silence and aloud. Today it is to vision the sheep of all continents, of all colors, of all cultures. Some have found this message about the other sheep foremost material for speaking of Jesus Christ to "others." It has opened the door to men of Africa, India, South America. These people came to sense that they were included in the worldwide flock of God's sheep.

"Verily, I say to you that ye are they of whom I said, 'Other sheep I have which are not of this fold; them also I must bring, and they shall hear my voice, and there shall be one fold and one shepherd.' And they understood me not, for they supposed it had been the Gentiles. . . . Ye are my sheep. . . . I have other sheep which are not of this land; neither of the land of Jerusalem; neither in any parts of that land round about where I have been to minister. . . . I have received a commandment of the Father, that I shall go to them, and that they may hear my voice, . . . that there may be one fold and one shepherd."—III Nephi 7:20 ff.

The Continuing Process of Learning

The Great Teacher expressed his teaching artistry on the Western continent. He had person-with-person association. He spoke in terms meaningful to the people. He limited his teaching to the scope of their comprehension and energy. One day he told his people that they had received as much as they could assimilate at that time. He told them, "I perceive . . . that you cannot understand all my words which I am commanded of the Father to speak unto you at this time." He told them to go to their homes and reflect upon what he had been saying, that they might "understand." They should prepare themselves for the morrow, for further teaching. He let his disciples know that their learning was to be an ever continuing experience. This accords with his counsel to his men during the Last Supper, "I have yet many things to say unto you, but ye cannot bear them now" (John 16:12).

The Covenanting in Baptism

Throughout the Book of Mormon man is pictured as designed by God to choose the course of his life. And choice is ever interpreted as involving acceptance of the consequences of one's choosing. God does not frighten persons into submission, does not hold them in ignorant subjection. He wants persons to choose with understanding. Jesus Christ employed baptism as the external expression of the inner choice that persons make. He expected that the whole person would be involved in the wholeness of God's work, in all God's universe. So he used the rite meaningful and familiar then and meaningful ever since: baptism by immersion. He expected that a person would "get in all over."

While Abinadi was speaking his message to King Noah and his priests, one young man caught the significance of what Abinadi was saying. This man Alma (Mosiah 9:1 ff.) had to flee for his life. Alma "went about privately among the people" and taught what he had learned from Abinadi. A small company of believers withdrew to a secluded place called "Mormon," where Alma interpreted baptism as Jesus gave meaning to it. He enlisted those who were "desirous to come into the fold of God"—to live together in mutual support and "to stand as witnesses of God at all times"—to be baptized and thereby express their covenanting. The record narrates the salutation made to Helam, a first convert, "Helam, I baptize you . . . as a testimony that you have entered into a covenant" with Jesus Christ. Helam was to live God's way and God was to grant Helam the sustaining ministry of the Holy Spirit (Mosiah 9:44). This was the connotation of baptismal covenanting that Jesus taught.

Jesus intended that this baptism should be a covenanting for forthright saints. He never promised living on Easy Street in Comfy Apartments. He never invited persons to join who held the attitude expressed by a young modern to his friend, "Give your heart to Jesus—it won't hurt you a bit." He had no place for the halfhearted disciple. A man was to be all for the Christ or outside the circle. He said right frankly, "No man can serve two masters" (III Nephi 5:115). The covenant was to be all-inclusive.

The Ministering of the Holy Spirit to the Covenanted

Jesus Christ was very specific in advising his disciples that he would be with them for a limited time. They would concentrate while he was with them and make ready to carry on after his departure. His provision for them after his leaving is more clearly presented in his farewell message to his men in the Upper Room in Jerusalem. There he was laying groundwork for what they would be doing after his leaving them. What he had been giving them in direct personal ministry would be continued in the ministry of the Holy Spirit, the Comforter. This ministry would afford "comfort"—that is, strength. It would provide instruction, guidance, and companionship. Sometimes there would be commendation, sometimes rebuke. This ministry would be conditioned by their capacity, their response, their utilization of this endowment in their ministry. And this ministry of the Holy Spirit would function above social restrictions and geographical distance.

Jesus Christ promised the ministry of the Holy Spirit to his disciples after their covenanting, which ministry would continue after his departing. He prayed, "Father, I pray thee that thou wilt give the Holy Ghost to all them that shall believe in their words" (III Nephi 9:21).

Mormon wrote farewell counsel to his son Moroni and spoke of the functioning of the Holy Spirit in effecting transforming fruitage in the lives of believers. This Spirit was much more than some ephemeral trimming, some spectacular overt outburst. This Spirit was to be fruit-bearing in personal living. Mormon spoke of "firstfruits." He put it this way, "Because of meekness and lowliness of heart comes the visitation of the Holy Ghost, which Comforter fills with hope and perfect love" (Moroni 8:29). In a previous letter Mormon designated "charity" as the basic fruit of the ministry of the Holy Spirit and identified this charity as "the pure love of Christ" (Moroni 7:52). This is the earmark of the "true followers" of Jesus Christ. This charity distinguishes "the sons of God."

The Three Nephites

Here is an incident that can be lowered to presumptuous speculation or elevated to high level of mission. This is pictured as taking place during Jesus Christ's leave-taking. He asked his disciples (presumably his twelve) "one by one" what they desired most of him after he should leave. All but three said that they wanted, after they had "lived to the age of man," to be with Christ in his kingdom. The three said nothing. Christ discerned what they were thinking, and he said to them, "Ye have desired that ye might bring the souls of men to me while the world shall stand" (III Nephi 13:21). These three were more concerned with what they could give than with what they might get. They wanted to keep on ministering for the good of others. So he promised that they should continue ministering and that they should have "fullness of joy." This would be the kind of joy designated in Doctrine and Covenants 16:3. This is the joy that is not concerned with rewards but with spiritual companionship with fellow disciples, with God. In this sense the incident of the blessing of "the three Nephites" stands high.

The Community of Brothers in Christ

The fruitage of Jesus Christ's ministry is narrated in IV Nephi 1:1-21. Here is the picture of a community bonded together in this charity of Christ. Nephites and Lamanites joined in common faith, in mutual love. The writer of IV Nephi explains it all this way: "The love of God did dwell in the hearts of the people." There were no divisions: "They were in one, the children of God." Then follows this soul-stirring comment about the community united in Jesus Christ, in all phases of living together: "And surely there could not be a happier people among all the people who had been created by the hand of God" (IV Nephi 1:19).

During its functioning an expanding community, an evangelistic nucleus, was reaching out to include more and more. Here was a Zion for ministering to all the world for the universal Christ.

Considerations for Conversation

1. Evaluate and expand this comment: "The Book of Mormon helps us appreciate that the ministry of Jesus Christ was and is for all the world."

2. What is your reaction to the observation that the sayings of Jesus Christ in the Book of Mormon are pretty much the same as those in the gospels of the New Testament?

3. From the practical standpoint of the everyday affair of making a living, how would it have been impracticable for Jesus Christ to have stayed a much longer time with the Nephites?

4. How does the ministry of Jesus Christ as told in III Nephi express qualities that make him the "Great Teacher"? Give examples.

5. What incidents express how Jesus reached out to persons as person, by name rather than by number, in face-to-face contacts? (See III Nephi 5:18; 8:70, 73; 13:12 ff, 8:23.)

6. What insights about the nature, the purpose, the

method of ministering are disclosed in Jesus Christ's calling, directing, and using his men? What do you see as his motivation and method of ministering?

7. From what Jesus said and did, what do you see as the purpose of "the church"? How did he proceed in developing the church? Did he hold an organization meeting? What did Jesus Christ mean by "the church" as he proceeded to define what the church was in ancient America?

8. One day Jesus Christ said, "This is my gospel" (III Nephi 12:34). Go through his ministry, his teachings in III Nephi, and indicate what you consider he meant his gospel to be.

9. How are you going to use the teaching about "the other sheep" in furthering our evangelistic fraternity in all the world today?

10. How is the picture expressed in IV Nephi 1:1-21 the outcome that should take place in the period after the ministry of Jesus Christ? What constituted Zionic living? How did deterioration of the community come to take place?

11. How would you help a person not familiar with the Book of Mormon lay a foundation for reading the story of the advent and ministry of Jesus Christ as it begins with III Nephi 5? What would you accentuate?

Exploration V. The Book Speaks of Family Living . . . The good family lines up and lives with God. The family pictured is Hebrew in tone, in operation. The question is never whether there are to be families but what kind of family life there is going to be.

Not long ago a youth said he would like to read the Book of Mormon and find out how a several-wives family would operate. He said he had always wondered how such a family resolved daily problems. He concluded by saying, "Wow, that ought to be interesting reading!" His friend, a Latter Day Saint youth, responded, "I think you would find this Book of Mormon pretty dull. There isn't anything in it that talks about what you are interested in." Replied the friend, "Isn't that the book that gave the Mormons their notions about having two, three, or more wives?" The response, "I do not know where the Mormon leaders got their notions about polygamy, but they didn't get them out of the Book of Mormon. It is a one-wife book." This comment led to the next query, "Does this Book of Mormon have anything to say about any kind of family living?"

Out of the General Story

There are no chapters on family living as such. Yet

concern for and reference to family operation runs throughout the book. Everywhere in the Book of Mormon family relationships are held as highly important. Not any kind of family will do. God is the central, uniting figure in home living held as ideal. Marriage is assumed to be the God-intended way for humans. And having children is pictured as the way God intends for man. There is no discount of sex: there is emphasis on the wholesome, considerate expression of sex. The picture ideal is that of mutual love.

With a Jewish Background

The migrants from Jerusalem brought their patterns and their ideals for the family. The Jews are heralded throughout history as foremost in exalting and maintaining the family as the primary group in their civil and religious living. Many of their festivals and holy days centered in the family and entailed family expression. The Sabbath was ushered in by the family and observed by the family. "Keeping the Sabbath" was always a family matter. Observance of the Passover stands to the fore. The Passover meal was eaten by the family group. In the narration of the first Passover a younger member of the family asked what all the observance meant and a senior member told the story. Some festivals of later origin, such as Hanukkah, had not yet emerged at the times of Book of Mormon migrations.

The way the Jews believed in their God made a great difference in their family living. The adage, "Show me the way a family believes in God and you will show me what kind of family life they will have," is applicable. The God of the Jews was orderly and purposeful. He was a worker. The command to his people to work six days of the week was as obligatory as the command to rest on the seventh day and remember and revere God. The Jewish notion of a "chosen people" carried over to notions of a "chosen family" with sense of assignment in God's work. Their conviction that God is righteous had strong implications for conduct in family living. Members of the family were to be righteous. Often they needed to be reminded that there was one code of righteousness and that this applied to their relations with both fellow Jews and Gentiles. Certainly the righteousness that God required was to apply to family relationships.

Jewish culture gave certain priority to the male. God was pictured as masculine. There was no mother god. The husband-father was the patriarch of the family group. There was a certain priority assigned to the male child over the female child. There was rejoicing when the firstborn was a son. Women held an important yet somewhat secondary status. And there was considerable variety in the patriarchal fathers that came to be. Some would be the big-boss type; some would be the hear-grandfather brand; some would be the kind, firm father type. Occasionally there would be the what's-it-to-me kind of man.

The Book of Mormon is honest enough to recognize and present the several types of fathers. On one side is King Benjamin who lived with and taught his three sons that they might "become men of understanding" (Mosiah 1:3). He taught them in living the way of working with God. On the other side were the profligate priests of Noah who in time of danger deserted their wives and their children and fled (Mosiah 9:86). Then they captured some Lamanite young women for new wives (Mosiah 9:111). The book is pretty clear concerning the type of family living held up as desirable.

God Is Portrayed and Addressed as Father

The Hebrews used the highest expression of social relationship that they knew when they identified God. These

Western-world Jews did not often refer to God by a name. The term Jehovah is used only two times in the book. Once a psalm is quoted, "Jehovah is my strength and my song!" (II Nephi 9:133). The other use is in the closing verse of the book. But "Father" keeps occurring. Early in I Nephi (3:217) this question is presented, "Remember thou the covenants of the Father unto the house of Israel?" Here is reference to the covenanting relationship between God as father and his sons and daughters. There is implication that this is to be the nature of the relationship in the family.

Jesus kept emphasizing this Father-son relationship. He told his disciples to love one another, even to love their enemies, "That you may be the children of your Father" (III Nephi 5:91). Loving relationship with the Father and all his children was given as the way of family living in all of life, and certainly in the domestic family. Jesus told his disciples of God's understanding and continuing love: "Your heavenly Father knows that you have need of all these things" (III Nephi 6:10). This kind of perceptive and providing love would characterize the relationship of the father in a family with his sons and daughters. What is more, Jesus lived this life in communion with his own Father. So should parents and their children commune, freely, frankly, faithfully.

When Moroni rounds out and abridges his writings he used this portrait of God. In the prayer of blessing on the bread and the wine, there are no high-sounding salutations of adoration that put God far away and "over there." God is saluted as "eternal Father." There is a covenanting between him and his sons. And God is promising to be with his covenanting children; the disciples pray "that they may always have his Spirit to be with them" (Moroni 4:4). We may think of the Father and his sons and daughters sharing a companionable meal together. Such is the suggestion for the good family.

The First Family Camp in America

When good King Benjamin was old, he instructed his son Mosiah to bring together his people for a farewell message from the king. He would turn over the kingship to his son. What eventuated was a family camp. All members of the family came to the capital city. This was the description of what happened:

"When they came up to the temple, they pitched their tents round about, every man according to his family, consisting of his wife, and his sons, and his daughters, and their sons, and their daughters, from the eldest down to the youngest, every family being separate, one from another."—Mosiah 1:33.

Some adjustments were required that the people might hear the king, for the camp came to be pretty large; but the family remained the unit. And the king talked to his people as a father would converse with children he loved. He called them "my friends and my brothers, my kindred and my people" (Mosiah 2:7).

The reaction to what the king said was so deep, so pervasive, that the people wanted to give expression to their feelings. They volunteered, "We are willing to enter into a covenant with our God, to do his will" (Mosiah 3:6). To this King Benjamin replied, "Now, because of the covenant which you have made, you shall be called the children of Christ, his sons, and his daughters" (3:8). The nation as a family joined, each by name; only the small children did not enter into the covenant. When the family camp closed, "They returned every one according to their families, to their own houses" (Mosiah 4:4).

A Husband-Wife Companionship

Jacob, a younger brother of Nephi ben Lehi, spoke out vehemently about the kind of family life his people should have. There was no place for sensuous motivation or for social advantage through having multiple wives. Each family was to be a husband-wife companionship. He thundered out against the harems of David and Solomon with their many wives and concubines (Jacob 2:33 ff.). And "whoredom" in the sense of lewd and promiscuous sex relations was expressly forbidden.

Jacob was very perceptive in his denunciation of plural marriage. He went further than saying that it was "wrong." He pointed out what this kind of family life would do to the members of the family. He said that God had heard "the cries of the fair daughters of this people." They were victims of this kind of family living. He denounced his people, saying they had "done greater iniquity than the Lamanites." This was his charge: "You have broken the hearts of your tender wives, and have lost the confidence of your children because of your bad examples before them; and the sobbings of their hearts ascend up to God against you."

What Jacob said next must have struck hard at his own people. He dared say that the Lamanites were doing better in their family living than were the Nephites. This was his forthright charge:

> "Behold, the Lamanites, your brethren, whom you hate . . . are more righteous than you. For they have not forgotten the commandments of the Lord, which were given our fathers, that they should have save it were one wife, and concubines they should have none, and there should not be whoredoms committed among them. . . . Their husbands love their wives, and their wives love their husbands, and their husbands and their wives love their children."—Jacob 2:54-57.

Jacob pleaded with his people for improved conditions in family living. He charged them to refrain from reviling against the Lamanites "because of their filthiness." Rather were they to look to their own filthiness. He closed with this injunction, "Remember your own children and [consider] how you have grieved their hearts because of the example that you have set before them" (Jacob 2:62).

Family Deterioration in Noah's Day

Noah was the son of Zeniff who had led a group of Nephites back to the land they had inhabited before they withdrew to get away from the Lamanites. In a comparatively short while this colony of Zeniff had been troubled and oppressed by the Lamanites. When Zeniff became old he conferred his kingdom upon one of his sons, Noah. This Noah was described as a man who "did walk after the desires of his own heart" (Mosiah 7:2). This summary sentence says much: "He had many wives and concubines" (7:3). He laid a heavy tax upon his people in order "to support himself and his wives and his concubines, and also his priests and their wives and their concubines." This polygamous program called for the construction of "many elegant and spacious buildings" with ornate furnishings. He built a "spacious palace" for himself and his harem, with elaborate throne and throne room. He pushed the planting of vineyards for the production of "wine in abundance." So King Noah "placed his heart upon his riches, and he spent his time in riotous living with his wives and his concubines" (7:20). So did his priests. The colony collapsed under such carrying on. When values for family living went down, the nation went down.

The Family, a Goal for National Liberty

War between the Nephites and the Lamanites kept

recurring. Some five hundred years after their arrival in the Western land the monarchy came to a close with the death of King Mosiah (Mosiah 13:67). About two decades later the Lamanites bore down upon the Nephites. The chief captain of the military forces of the Nephites was Moroni, a stalwart fellow of twenty-five years. He was a clever strategist and he was also a man of spiritual integrity. He challenged his people to fight for what they valued most. This was the estimate in the record:

> "The Nephites were inspired by a better cause; for they were not fighting for monarchy nor power. But they were fighting for their homes, and their liberties, their wives, and their children, . . . for their rites of worship and their church. . . .
>
> "The Lord had said, 'Ye shall defend your families, even to bloodshed'; therefore were the Nephites contending with the Lamanites, to defend themselves, and their families, and their lands, and their country, and their rights, and their religion."—Alma 20:50, 52.

When the Lamanites turned on the Nephites with savage onslaught, Moroni inspired his people to extra effort, to further courage by reminding them of the values they were defending. They were fighting for their faith, for their families.

The Title of Liberty

Captain Moroni had to face internal dissension. A dissenter arose by the name of Amalickiah. He was described as "a large and strong man" who "was desirous to be a king" and who pushed his way by promises and "flatteries." The situation was described as "exceedingly precarious and dangerous, notwithstanding their great victory which they had had over the Lamanites." Moroni was well aware of the danger. This time he "rent his coat" and took a piece and wrote on it the slogan for his fight, "In memory of our God, our religion, our freedom, our peace, our wives, our children!" He posted this banner on a pole that countrymen might see. Then he girded himself with his full armor and hoisted the pole with its banner which he called "the title of liberty" (Alma 21:41, 42). He "prayed mightily" and then went forth with his banner, calling his people to covenant to stand for these rights designated on "the title of liberty." His people rallied. His people convenanted. Amalickiah fled. Then Captain Moroni "caused the title of liberty to be hoisted upon every tower which was in all the land" (21:71). The Nephites had rallied to save their faith and their families.

Specialization of Function in Family Living

Members of a family had their own roles and their own functions. In some families there are parasite members, in some there are servile members. In times of social change the roles of members may become pretty confused. The Book of Mormon does not uphold lazy loiterers or selfish spongers. Industry is a virtue. Every person works to make some contribution. Zeniff recorded how his people got along until they were molested by the Lamanites, until priests and princes came to think of themselves as persons of privilege. This was his picture of labor assignments.

> "And I did cause that the men should till the ground, and raise all manner of grain, and all manner of fruit, of every kind. And I did cause that the women should spin, and toil, and work all manner of fine linen; yea, and cloth of every kind, that we might clothe our nakedness; and thus we did prosper in the land."— Mosiah 6:31-33.

Some sixty years after the initiation of the judgeship

government, there came a period of peace. Many Lamanites turned toward God with "firmness and steadiness in faith" (Helaman 2:118). The two peoples "did fellowship one with another" (2:121). This was the picture of their fields of specialized endeavor: They worked all kinds of ore and refined it. They raised grain in abundance, both in the north and in the south. They raised many flocks and herds, many fatlings. Their women "did toil and spin, and did make all manner of cloth."

The Secondary Place of Things and Things

The Book of Mormon never discounts material things. It does, however, always place these in the supportive role. Persons and their spiritual expression here have first place. Always it is clear that material things are secondary and are to be contributive to spiritual family living. Whenever things take control, family decline follows.

The condition of the Zoramites speaks significantly. Ammon and some co-workers went to the Zoramites (Alma 81 ff.). In their prosperity they had become confident of their superiority and their favor with God. They gloried that they were not as other people. Alma caught their scale of values and made this observation about what was happening in them.

> "Behold, O my God, their costly apparel, and their ringlets, and their bracelets, and their ornaments of gold, and all their precious things which they are ornamented with and, behold, their hearts are set upon them."—Alma 16:105.

These self-satisfied people "cast out of the synagogues" their countrymen who did not have such clothing and ornamentation. They ejected them "because of the coarseness of their apparel" (Alma 16:122). Alma saw how these people in all their living had lost the values that insure family living. In modern language we would say that children and companionship and charity had been relegated to inferior position while carpets and cameos, cars and clothes, cosmetics and coiffures, clubs and checking accounts had superseded.

Diversity and Discord in a Family

There is no one prevailing picture of what a family ought to be. There is no description of a family in which members are identicals. Rather is there the impression of diversity within the family and difference between families. There is respect for integrity of personhood. Each person is gauged in accordance with his stock of resources and the social situation.

The family of Lehi discloses problems, achievements, tragedies, differences. The clash between Nephi and his brothers Laman and Lemuel constitutes a domestic melee of high intensity, a conflict situation that was never resolved. The moralistic preacher is inclined to side completely with Nephi while the surveyor of human nature might say, "The older boys had a point." The Book of Mormon is honest enough to present the inability of the family to work together in common cause. In a conversation about this family one youth observed, "If I had been Laman I would have smacked Nephi down for his self-righteousness and his opinion that God was completely on his side." Another youth said, "Why didn't they leave these older boys in Jerusalem? They didn't want to leave their city and they didn't like being bossed by brother." Another commented, "Did Nephi have to take the lead? Was Father Lehi too weak?" The picture is so well presented that different opinions are possible. There were plenty of "murmurs" and plenty of complaints and plenty of revolts. All this sounds like a scene out of family living.

Eventually the family split in two. When Lehi died (II Nephi 3:23) the last force for unity was gone. Nephi became more expressive of the view, "God is on my side." The brothers came out in the open with, "Let's get rid of him!" They said, "We are not going to have our younger brother be our ruler!" (4:4). Nephi and his followers withdrew to a new location. Of their new way of life Nephi wrote, "It came to pass that we lived after the manner of happiness" (II Nephi 4:43). Was there any way this family might have resolved strain and difference?

Three Sons Not Identicals

Alma, son of Alma, would be called a "rebel" in modern times. He was "numbered among the unbelievers." He was a sampler of assorted ways of living. He had what moderns would call "a good line." He was gifted in flattery. He experienced a spiritual jolt (Mosiah 11:162 ff.) and was converted. His friends, the sons of Mosiah, followed him in both ways. The energy and the constancy of his life after his conversion is hardly describable. His awareness of what had taken place in his own life must have helped him to appreciate the diversity in his three sons.

In his later years he gave his sons their patriarchal blessings. They were individually directed, individually expressed as such blessings should be. The record says, "He caused that his sons should be gathered together that he might give unto them every one his charge, separately, concerning the things pertaining unto righteousness" (Alma 16:160). Then follow the counsels, one in each chapter, for Helaman, Shiblon, Corianton. Such differences in these three sons of Alma!

To Helaman and Shiblon Alma spoke in commendation and expectation. He committed them to their ministries and commended them to God. To Shiblon he could say, "I have had great joy in you already, because of your faithfulness and your diligence" (Alma 18:3). There is a different tone and theme with Corianton. This son had had some lost weekends among the Zoramites. He had got involved with "the harlot Isabel" who was pretty popular with many men. He calls this son to remember that "Wickedness never was happiness" (Alma 19:74). There is no cover-up in his counsel. Yet he comes right to the point and says, "You are called of God" (Alma 19:115). This understanding father did not give up. He believed that this son with such adventurous spirit would find his place. After Alma left the land of Zarahemla (Alma 21:20) Corianton is mentioned on the roster of ministers (Alma 21:185). The last mention of him was to do with his voyage "northward, in a ship, to carry forth provisions" to the people who had migrated to that land (Alma 30:14). Apparently he closed his life on a venture of service.

Alma's insight into the nature of his three sons constitutes a contributing picture in family diversity and family unity.

Jesus Christ Ministered to Families

When the Nephites assembled to meet with Jesus Christ, all members of the family came. The multitude included all age groups. After Jesus had been teaching his people for a long while, he told them, "Go to your homes, and ponder upon the things which I have said." He advised them to pray that they might understand, that they might prepare their minds for teaching the next day. The family was to be the conversational, devotional group.

Jesus Christ made "the multitude" a family circle in which he blessed the "little children" (III Nephi 8:12 ff.). There was no mass ritualism. "He took their little children, one by one, and blessed them" (verse 23). This was the nature of all his meetings and sacraments. When he closed the meeting, "The multitude dispersed, and every man took his wife and his children and returned to his own home" (III Nephi 9:1).

Considerations for Conversation

1. On what basis did Jacob denounce plural marriage? What did he imply was the effect on members of the family? How would you interpret polygamy as undesirable to persons of a contemporary culture who practice it?

2. What were some of the dangers that threatened family living in Book of Mormon times? Were these in persons or in society? What dangers threaten the family in contemporary times?

3. What was the role of the wife-mother in the Book of Mormon story? Was there any uncertainty about this? How is this a problem in contemporary society?

4. What do you see as factors in the Lehi family that got in the way of harmonious family living? What responsibility for this strain and hostility might be placed on Lehi, on Sariah, on Nephi, on Laman, on the adopted members of the family party?

5. Did the Lehi family have conferences or preaching meetings? What might have been the agendum for a family conference? What guidelines do you set forth for conducting family conferences today?

6. The Book of Mormon speaks much of the essentiality of "charity, the pure love of Christ." What are qualities of this kind of love? How does this differ from some contemporary conceptions of love? What kind of love is conducive to effective family living?

7. How was industry and workmanship considered

essential in Book of Mormon family living? Under what conditions do you consider industry and workmanship assets in family living? When liabilities?

8. In the Book of Mormon Jesus Christ told his disciples, "Pray in your families unto the Father." From his inclusive ministry of teaching and praying, what do you see as guidelines for fruitful family praying? (See III Nephi 8:52) How would praying in the family be commendable and fruitful and when would it be otherwise? What is the significance of the counsel that Jesus gave to his disciples "that they should not cease to pray in their hearts"? (III Nephi 9:38)

9. What examples do you find in the Book of Mormon that express how "a family does things together"? What are some worthful things that a modern family can do together? How might mere doing things get in the way of a high quality of family living? How does a family "do things together with God"?

10. How would a family camp of our times differ from the family camp in King Benjamin's times? What would the two have in common?

11. What conception or operation of God as Father is sound and helpful in family living in which God is considered a member of the family? How would the conception of God as father affect the conception of the father in the family?

12. How may the salutation "our Father" affect the living of a family in today's world, in today's church?

Exploration VI. The Book Predicts the Ministry of the Holy Spirit . . . Writers do not discuss and interpret the ministry of the Spirit. This ministry is assumed as essential, as ever available. Jesus Christ enabled richer experience.

Here "predicate" denotes the affirming of something without saying much about it. What is predicated is seen as self-evident. It is considered to be clear enough, accepted enough that supporting explanations and "proofs" are not needed. Yet what is predicated is considered indispensable. In such cases we do not expect to find quotations and arguments. For instance, when a man builds his life on foundations of honesty, he does not parade his integrity and he does not argue about what honesty is. He simply lives honestly and assumes that this is the good way to live. It is not unlikely that the man who likes to discriminate between fine points and draw up statements and resolutions about honesty might be somewhat wobbly in his own patterns of honest living. In the case of a book, as in the case of a person, we have to see the whole book in order to discern its predications.

The Book of Mormon Predicates

This book has no systematic consideration of the nature

and ministry of the Holy Spirit. The theologian who wants an organized statement of doctrine will be disappointed. There is little to quote. The person who likes to go through the book and mark quotations will not find much that will satisfy him. Such use of the Book of Mormon is hardly to be recommended. One has to live in the book as a whole and feel its life, its message. Then occasionally a certain passage may be seen as expressing the quintessence of the inclusive message. This applies to our exploration about the ministry of the Holy Spirit. We have to see the whole book with its continuing message.

Yet the Book of Mormon presumes throughout its story that the Holy Spirit is basic in man's living with God and in God's providing for man. Reference to this ministry runs throughout the record although there may be no specific designating. It might be said that the working of the Holy Spirit is taken for granted, that the purpose and function are presumed. The silence of the book in matters of quotations and directives implies predicating of importance.

This silence may be due to different factors. One view is caught up in the phrase, "Of course you know all about this." Another view may be, "We have no language for talking about this." This is ever a problem. In modern life religionists are bothered because they have no "God language" for talking about God in terms meaningful and adequate for today's thought world. There has always been lack of "Spirit language" for talking about the Holy Spirit. And this great lack is disturbing us today. Our church is faced with the need to acquire such language. So the Book of Mormon refers to Spirit-guided and Spirit-enlivened experiences without diagnosing them, without interpreting them. Then, too, there is the viewpoint held by some that such matters are too sacred for examination. In this light we remember what Socrates said, "Unexamined life is not worth living." And many of us living today are saying, "Unexamined spirituality is not safe for living." At least we can say that in the book the Holy Spirit is predicated. This power whether called Spirit or Ghost is considered indispensable.

From First to Last in the Book

Sometimes Christians give the impression that the Holy Spirit was something that happened for the first time on the Day of Pentecost. They imply that this was first discussed when Jesus was conversing with his men in his farewell counsel during the Last Supper (see John 15, 16). They seem to consider that the ministry of the Holy Spirit belongs only to the Christian Era.

The Book of Mormon does not support this assumption. The first book in the collection of writings (I Nephi) speaks of "the Spirit" and the closing chapter of the last book, Moroni, speaks of "the power of the Holy Ghost." References, direct and indirect, continue throughout the story. The first chapter of the book relates how Lehi "was filled with the Spirit of the Lord" (I Nephi 1:11) as he perceived the impending destruction of Jerusalem and as he accepted his own assignment to lead his family away from the city. Later when King Benjamin was giving his farewell message to his countrymen, he called his people to repentance, to rededication to their calling. This is the record of what happened: "The Spirit of the Lord came upon them, and they were filled with joy" (Mosiah 2:5). This was a long time and a long distance from the scene of the Day of Pentecost.

The Book of Mormon predicates the Spirit of God as inherent in God's continuing, ongoing program. There is no beginning and no end to the expression of this spiritual dynamic. What recorders look upon as beginnings, as "firsts," are happenings in the ever moving stream of life in which God and man are engaged together. The Spirit of God is eternally functioning. Man can come into relationship and man can get out of relationship with God, so man may or may not experience this ministry. There is no discontinuance on God's part; there may be lack of readiness, lack of communication, on man's part. The Spirit of God is eternal. This is the predication of the Book of Mormon.

With Diverse Terminology

The terms Holy Ghost and Holy Spirit are used synonymously in the Nephite record. For instance in II Nephi 15:1 Nephi speaks of "the Holy Ghost," and in the next verse he speaks of "the Holy Spirit." In Moroni 10:5, 7, there is mention of "the Holy Ghost." A few verses later (10:9, 10) is reference to "the Spirit of God." A little later the term "the Spirit of Christ" is used (verse 12). Sometimes the simple phrase "the Spirit" is used (Moroni 8:33). There is no one set of phrasings, no disposition to limit God to conventional phrasings. The Book of Mormon does not strain concerning differences and uses interchangeably "Holy Ghost," "Holy Spirit," and "Spirit of God."

Persons with expanding realization of God's nature and ways are inclined to be humble in applying names and phrases and concepts to God and his universe. These persons realize that any language resources they have are inadequate when it comes to describing and designating God. They are ever wanting more adequate means for speaking of God and for speaking of the Holy Spirit. The Book of Mormon used what language was available. Today we need to re-express its predications in terms and in experiences more meaningful for our time. We are more inclined to speak of the Holy Spirit than the Holy Ghost since the latter term, for many persons, carries associations and connotations that veer from the truly spiritual. For instance one boy asked if we could have more of the Holy Ghost at Halloween. We are always needing more descriptive means of indicating what takes place when the Spirit of God functions in our living. We are conscious that we are trying to designate something whose reality is richer than our words can ever express.

The New Testament Writings Came Later

The New Testament manuscripts had not been written when Jesus Christ visited the Western continent. Those events narrated in the Book of Acts and in the epistles of Paul had not yet taken place. It is wise to read what is said in the closing books of the Book of Mormon and then proceed to the writings of Luke and John and Paul. These are the men who wrote about the ministerings of the Holy Spirit. They spoke of the vitalizing, unifying, commissioning influence of this Spirit. They set forth norms for evaluating the ministering of the Spirit. Paul is pretty clear in indicating that some so-called expressions are shallow, others spurious. Yet always he predicates the indispensability of this ministry. For him the church is a Spirit-endowed fellowship with mission.

The New Testament writings continue this emphasis on the ministering of the Spirit and on the fruitage of love that comes through this ministering. The curtain falls on the scenes in the life of a Spirit-led movement. During centuries that followed there was decline in matters of spiritual endowment. The notion grew that spiritual unction was to come through institutionalized procedures and the officiation of priests of what we might call "the Establishment." There came to be little talking about "the Spirit of God." Rather there was talking about "the grace of God" limited to its administration in prescribed ways. What happened in the New Testament in the ministerings and the miracles of the Holy Ghost became a memory.

A Need in Contemporary Life

Moderns tend to put quotation marks around "the Spirit" and "the Holy Ghost." Often moderns are inclined to give the words an inflection that does not speak approval. The inflection may be quizzical or discounting. There is frequent tendency to confuse misconception and mispractice with weakness and fallacy in the thing itself. Often "the Spirit" is associated with extremists and fanatics.

Yet in recent years there has been more reference to the Holy Spirit than formerly. More has been printed about the Spirit. This is significant when we note that the creeds of the Reformation were silent about the Holy Spirit. This was not a concern of those times, so nothing had to be formulated about it. It is different today. So we ask, What does the Book of Mormon have to say about the Holy Spirit? Can the book give us any guidance for today's living?

Are There Two Categories for Spirit Ministry?

Some legalists are inclined to split the ministering of the Holy Spirit into two categories with differing titles for them. Some say, for instance, that the Spirit of God may be experienced by persons before they are baptized but that they may not receive the Holy Ghost, for this is restricted to those who have been baptized and confirmed. Such a differentiation is hardly true to the nature of God. God does not function in such divisions, in such breaks. His ministering is ever in a single process, differentiated according to the fitness, persons, and situations. And God does not arrange for some rite such as baptism to make a distinct breach in his ministerings.

The Book of Mormon gives the impression that God's spiritual resources are available to every person according to his fitness, his capacity, his responsiveness, his wisdom, his inclination to use them. Baptism is to help qualify a person for additional spiritual endowment by reason of covenanting with God, of changing the pattern of living, of becoming immersed in God's work and way of life. And confirmation is designed to further life-with-life contact with God. The ministry of hands expresses this person-with-person coming together. The Book of Mormon has no splitting of this ministry into two distinct parts, with one term for the ministry before baptism and another term for the ministry after baptism. It can affirm with Paul, "There is one Spirit" (Ephesians 4:4).

This Spirit Is for All!

Moroni wrote good counsel about the universal availability of the Spirit. There are no special privileges to this class or this clan or this color. God provides the universal availability. He leaves to every person the choosing of response. Such person-with-person influence cannot be legislated or compelled. There is suggestion that God affords availability to every man, leaving the responding in type and degree to the condition of the person. The closing book says,

> "The Spirit of Christ is given to every man that he
> may know good from evil; wherefore I show you the
> way to judge: for everything which invites to do good,
> and persuades to believe in Christ is sent forth by the
> power and gift of God."—Moroni 7:14.

This is saying what John wrote about this same power, which he calls "the true light, which lighteth every man who cometh into the world" (John 1:9).

When Two Cultures Met

The Book of Mormon speaks of the outreaching ministry

of the Holy Spirit with drawing power and regenerating influence. There is outstanding expression of this in the Spirit-enlivened missionary ministry among the Lamanites. The God of the Nephite missionaries was also the God of the Lamanite converts. And the Good Spirit ministered to both. When Ammon, the Nephite, stood before Lamoni, the Lamanite, this king was aware of the spiritual empowerment that attended Ammon. The record says that Ammon was "filled with the Spirit of God" so that he was able to discern the reactions and thoughts of the king. In bewilderment King Lamoni asked, "Are you the Great Spirit who knows all things?" (Alma 12:93). This is apropos these days when one world religion comes in contact with another. Believers in different faiths can feel together the pull of the Infinite, of the Eternal that we may call "the Great Spirit." Ammon was alert and discerning. He did not deny or denounce what the Lamanite had said. He identified Lamoni's "Great Spirit" with his own God who ministered through his "Good Spirit." Then Ammon continued with explanation the king would understand:

> "I am a man; and man in the beginning was created after the image of God, and I am called by his Holy Spirit to teach these things to this people that they may be brought to a knowledge of that which is just and true. And a portion of that Spirit dwelleth in me, which giveth me knowledge, and also power, according to my faith and desires which are in God."—Alma 12:112-113.

The following is a broad portrayal of the functioning of the Holy Spirit in Ammon's experience: (1) Insight into the needs of another; (2) intent to uplift others and bring them to God for good life; (3) appreciation of man as person designed in the image of God; (4) overview of God's plan and purpose for man; (5) awareness of the redemptive love of

God for all; and (6) strength and courage to witness for God. Ammon pointed out clearly that in him was "a portion of that Spirit." In him there could be an increasing or a diminishing portion. There was significance in his use of the word "dwells." In his life in a fruit-producing way this Spirit was residing, functioning. This was not a sensational come-and-go visitation for a few high moments. This was for continuing development and deportment. Ammon was a Spirit-endowed minister.

In a quite different way this Spirit affected Lamoni, the king. He was overcome as was Paul on the Damascus road. Apparently the king needed a strong spiritual jolt. His own sense of unworthiness entered into his undoing. He collapsed as if dead. This is clear: God did not wait to touch the Lamanite with the Spirit of God until he was baptized and confirmed. God started with Lamoni where he was, as he was.

This story helpfully summarizes Ammon's insight into the ministering of the Good Spirit. There was more than physical collapse. The light of God, the "marvelous light of his goodness," was shining into the king's personhood. "And, this light had infused such joy into his soul [that] the cloud of darkness [was] dispelled" (Alma 12:133-134). The Spirit of God was effecting conversion and transformation. This spiritual influence spread through the court. It was the succinct report of Ammon that he saw "the Spirit of the Lord poured out according to his prayers upon the Lamanites, his brothers" (verse 145).

The worthy outcome of this concentrated experience was expressed in what took place in the lives of those affected by the ministering of the Holy Spirit. Their own testimony was "that their hearts had been changed, that they had no more desire to do evil" (Alma 12:176). This was the summary statement of what took place.

> "As many as believed were baptized; and they became a righteous people, and they established a church among them. Thus the work of the Lord commenced among the Lamanites; thus the Lord began to pour out his Spirit upon them. And we see that his arm is extended to all people who will repent and believe on his name."

All this was a long while before the coming of Jesus Christ to the Nephite land. God was not on spiritual recess as far as the ministry of the Holy Spirit was concerned. God wished to draw to him all who would respond. Jesus Christ would be coming in reconciling and redeeming ministry to help persons get with God and to qualify for further spiritual ministry. These people sensed something of "the Spirit of Christ" before he came in person.

This Good Spirit effected a miracle in the relations of persons. Lamoni and Ammon became spiritual brothers. When the senior king of the Lamanites, the father of King Lamoni, met the two men he would have hewed down the Nephite and he wanted his son to get rid of this invader. In a short while he became aware of the genuine love that Ammon had for Lamoni. He was "astonished exceedingly!" (Alma 12:211). The Spirit of God had effected mighty changes.

Filled with Fire

Jesus Christ did not play up spectacular scenes. He did not broadcast news-making miracles. He was concerned with what was taking place in the lives of persons. He told his covenanting disciples that they should be "filled with the Holy Ghost, and with fire" (III Nephi 9:14). This fire was not a spiritual bomb explosion or a whopper bonfire. It was inner fire that would cleanse and warm for growth. There was light with this warmth. Jesus told his followers that after repentance and baptism, they should "be sanctified by the reception of the Holy Ghost" (III Nephi 12:33). These persons would be purified and totally consecrated to God.

The New Community

After Jesus Christ made his final departure, his disciples moved out on evangelistic mission. They went out as gospel ambassadors "to all people upon the face of the land" (III Nephi 13:35), and the Spirit was with them. Many were baptized and "They received the Holy Ghost." Then in spiritual chain reaction these newly covenanted disciples went out to witness. Both Nephites and Lamanites were baptized. The life of the resulting Zionic community is described in the first chapter of IV Nephi. Moroni described the spiritual quality of the community life. Those who were baptized "were wrought upon and cleansed by the power of the Holy Ghost" (Moroni 6:4).

"And the church met together often to fast and to pray, and to speak one with another concerning the welfare of their souls. . . . Their meetings were conducted by the church after the manner of the working of the Spirit . . . for as the power of the Holy Ghost led them whether to preach or exhort, or to pray, or to supplicate, or to sing, even so it was done."—Moroni 6:6, 9.

Jesus Christ Focused on Oneness

When Jesus was praying in the company of his men during the Last Supper in Jerusalem, he was concerned that his men see how his life was revealing what his Father was like. He wanted his men to see how he was revealing the very nature of God. It must have been painful for him when Philip asked him to show them the Father: "Show us the

Father, Lord, and we shall be satisfied." Jesus replied with some distress, "Have I been so long with you, Philip, without your really knowing me? The man who has seen me has seen the Father" (John 14:8 ff.). He prayed that his men would be one, would be one with him, as he and his Father were one. Jesus was concerned about this oneness when he was instructing his disciples on the Western continent. One day when he was talking about the salutation for baptism he said, "The Father, and the Son, and the Holy Ghost are one." The baptismal salutation might be considered an affirmation of this oneness. He went on to say, "I am in the Father, and the Father in me, and the Father and I are one" (III Nephi 5:27). Later he added, "The Father, and I, and the Holy Ghost are one" (5:38).

The words Jesus gave them for the baptism salutation are simple and meaningful in any culture. They could be addressed to Nathaniel of Galilee or Mathoni of Land Bountiful in ancient times, to Humberto of Mexico or Abrahama of Tahiti in these days. Each would hear in his own language, "Having authority given me of Jesus Christ, I baptize you in the name of the Father, and of the Son, and of the Holy Ghost. Amen." With English-speaking people the phrase would close with "of the Holy Ghost." With German-speaking Saints we would hear, "Heiligen Geistes." With Spanish-speaking Saints we would hear, "del Espiritu Santo." This oneness in wording can symbolize our oneness in endowment and fraternity. Each of us can hear this in a strange language and join in spirit with others.

The Book of Mormon points to and expresses this spiritual oneness in the Father and the Son and in the Holy Spirit. This leads to oneness in us, with God.

Above Disputation and Speculation

Jesus was blunt in his counsel to avoid "disputations" in

these matters. Sense of oneness was to be achieved through living with God, loving with God, laboring with God. Speculation and disputation would not achieve this oneness. Jesus was not telling his disciples that they should refrain from thinking. He was saying that presumptions and polemics and pretensions would never bring about the ministering of the Holy Spirit. They would have to live with God understandingly, mutually.

Jesus Christ never outlines any theology about a Trinity, either in Judea and Galilee or in Land Bountiful. All this was spun out later. We cannot imagine him singing "God in three persons, blessed Trinity." Rather did Jesus give his Nephite disciples straightforward counsel while he was speaking of this oneness of Father, Son, Spirit! "There shall be no disputations among you, as there hath hitherto been; neither shall there be disputations among you concerning the points of my doctrine, as there hath hitherto been" (III Nephi 5:29). Jesus virtually told his disciples to leave out trying to differentiate between Father, Son, and Spirit. Rather were they to focus on their oneness. The voice of history points up that where speculation has been indulged in, where disputation has occurred with evident interest in argumentation, the result has been deadness and division. There is difference between earnest searching and ephemeral speculation.

And what Spirit-language and what Spirit-heritage would they have for their exploration? Today we are still needing Spirit-language.

Basics Concerning the Holy Spirit

Since there are no treatises in the Book of Mormon about the Holy Spirit, we need to look into the book as a whole. In such an exploration, these basics stand forth:

1. The Holy Spirit eternally functions in the relationship of God with man. There has been no starting time for this ministry.

2. The ministering of the Holy Spirit is conditioned by man's capacity, his responsiveness, his wisdom, his integrity, his needs.

3. The Holy Spirit is expressed in diverse manifestations for the profit of man with bestowal of gifts conditioned by the nature and needs of the recipient and of others.

4. The ministry of the Holy Spirit can be reduced by the indifference and carelessness of men, by the institutionalism and misemphasis of the church.

5. The foremost fruit of the Holy Spirit is charity, the pure love of Christ. And this love is expressed in relationships.

6. The ministry of the Holy Spirit entails the spiritual development and transformation of persons and peoples.

7. The Spirit of Christ expressed in his life and personhood is the norm for the wholesome expression of the Holy Spirit.

Considerations for Conversation

1. Moroni wrote that the Spirit of God is granted to persons "to profit them" (10:9). In the total context what do you see as indicating what constitutes "profit"? How might this be misinterpreted?

2. What does a youth of our day mean when he says he would like to have language with which to consider the Holy Spirit; when he says that what he usually gets is quotations in another language?

3. How inclusive is your interpretation of "the truth of all things" as this phrase is used in Moroni 10:5? Some say this refers only to "spiritual things." What are "spiritual things"? Does this include biology as well as Bible, genetics as well as Genesis, sociology as well as sacraments?

4. What do you think Jesus meant when he told his disciples that they should be baptized "with fire and with the

Holy Ghost"? What meaning would "fire" convey? (III Nephi 5:46)

5. How do you see repentance and baptism as foundational for the enlarging experiencing of the Holy Spirit? How are these to function contributively?

6. What do you see as the process of exploration involved in the promise that "by the power of the Holy Ghost you may know the truth of all things"? (Micah 10:5) How much of our personhood is involved in "knowing"? How does the counsel given to Oliver Cowdery in 1829 apply? (See Doctrine and Covenants 9:3)

7. How and where does the Book of Mormon interpret the Holy Spirit as ministering to effect spiritual fraternity which is expandable to include all mankind?

8. In terms of oneness of humanity what is the significance of the foreview of things expressed in I Nephi 3:15? How did Paul meet this consideration?

9. How do you interpret to a friend-inquirer that the Spirit of God, the Holy Ghost, is reported throughout the book, even before the coming of Jesus Christ? What bearing does this have upon our conception of God's dealing with man? Note the mention even in the Book of Ether, as in Ether 1:105-106.

10. What thought-world did the Nephites have for considering the Holy Ghost? How did they interpret what this Spirit is and does? What is your thought-world for thinking about the Holy Spirit and interpreting this Spirit to our times?

11. When does a person have the right to expect that God will bestow on him "the gift and power of the Holy Ghost"? What obligations does reception entail? Who are persons in the Book of Mormon who were rightly blessed with the Spirit? How were they entitled to this blessing?

Exploration VII. The Book Speaks of the Mission of the Church . . . The church is considered a fellowship of disciples on mission. And Jesus Christ is the center, the source of power. Writers before the visitation by Christ use the term "church."

"Church" is a much used word in the Book of Mormon. Readers respond in two ways. One group welcomes the term and reads into it what they envision as "church." The other group considers that the word is out of place, for it was not used in ancient times. These look upon it as an invention of those who produced the book. Both need to get into the book and let it speak its own message. All need to see what the writers had in mind. And then we shall be able to see what the book has to say to us today. Certainly there is considerable "church" in the Book of Mormon.

The New Testament Word for Church

Generally we think of "church" as a New Testament word. The Greek work *ekklesia* was used by New Testament writers. This was a standard word, one much appreciated by the Greeks. On the whole it meant a convened assembly of free Greeks. Here citizens conversed, considered, sought common consent. In the earlier days their meetings opened with prayer and sacrifice. When the Christian writings were translated into the Latin, there was no attempt to change the word. *Ekklesia* was simply transliterated into *ecclesia.* In English the word "church" became the commonly used word, while we retained the original root in such words as ecclesiastical.

Yet there was something in Hebrew life and language that carried this notion of a convened and called assembly. The Hebrews used the word *quahal* to denote "assembly" or "congregation." For instance, in Leviticus 10:17 the Hebrew *quahal* which is expressed by *ekklesia* in the Septuagint translation (the Greek) is translated into English as "congregation." Both the Hebrews and the Greeks had words to indicate the coming together and living together of those who were bona fide members of their citizenry.

The Word for Joseph Smith

When Joseph Smith was translating and dictating copy for the Book of Mormon he had to use available terms meaningful to him. In this field his words were church and synagogue. The former is associated with the Christians, the latter with the Jews. Synagogue, like *ekklesia,* indicated an assembly of believing Jews in common faith and fellowship. Originally it meant the people, not the meetinghouse and this was true of "church."

Both terms came into use years after the Nephite migration from Jerusalem. Joseph Smith used these words because they carried the idea that he wanted to express. When we endeavor to designate something in a culture strange to us, we use the language symbols with which we are familiar. Sometimes we import words into another culture, words that are strange to the native folk of the culture. The word "corn" is found in the Bible. As a boy I visioned the kind of corn that I saw growing in central Iowa and presumed that this maize was grown in Judea. Later I thought that somebody had been toying with words, reading back into Canaan plant life something that did not belong there. Then I came to see that translators were doing the best they could and that "corn" meant grain that grew in a kernel. Joseph Smith used the word "church" because this simple word carried meaning.

Seeing With or Reading Into

We are ever inclined to read into a word what we are accustomed to see in the meaning we have of it. This applies to this word church. Conversation with Roman Catholics brings out how they think of "church" with its priesthood authority, its procedures, its phrasings. This holds for Mormons, Lutherans, and "Reorganites." We locate this word in the Book of Mormon and tend to read back into the meaning what we consider the word is to connote today. This is more marked because the Book of Mormon is our own book in our own church. Our meanings may include rites and sacraments, officers and administration, meetings and materials, doctrines and creeds, books and periodicals, and more. We conclude that church then was a duplicate of the church in our day, minus a few such things as pipe organs, printing presses, and computing machines.

It is imperative that we get the picture of "church" as originally expressed in the book. What in the book will contribute to our understanding and creating the church in our day? What was the church in Book of Mormon cultures? For what purpose did the church originate and continue?

The First Mention in the Book

The first use of the term church was in I Nephi, in the

first chapter. Nephi and his brothers had returned to Jerusalem to procure copy of some Jewish writings. Lehi wanted to be equipped with the scriptures of his people. He sensed the need for resources for continuity. Lehi's sons were instructed to go to the house of Laban. This eventuated in the death of Laban and the procurement of the records on plates of brass. After Nephi killed Laban he clothed himself in the garments of Laban and then commandeered the services of Laban's servant who mistook him for his master. Nephi told this servant that he wanted to carry the engravings which were on the plates of brass to his "elder brethren, who were without the walls" (I Nephi 1:127). Nephi directed the servant to follow him. When Nephi referred to his own brothers this servant of Laban presumed that his master Laban was referring to "the brethren of the church." In the conversation that followed, the servant referred to "the elders of the Jews" (I Nephi 1:130). Here church had a rather general meaning; it denoted the congregation of the Jews, with elders at the head.

The Church of the Courageous

Alma was converted through the courageous declarations of Abinadi. He was shown very forcibly that it took courage to be a true believer. Alma got out of the way of King Noah and his men, not from fear for his life but for intent to minister. He wanted to share with others the gospel he had come to know. So he "went about privately among the people, and began to teach the words of Abinadi" (Mosiah 9:28). In time he had to withdraw to a place called Mormon for solitude and safety. To this place came believers. A community, a congregation, took shape.

What took place at the waters of Mormon provides good index of the way a church comes to be. Such a group is a creation, a development, rather than an organization. There is no account of any organization meeting. There is no record of the calling or ordaining of Alma, but called he was. God was working directly with him. There could be no considerations of transmitted authority or of vote on his ordination. As in other cases, the man had to lead out as God directed him to do so. It was so with Isaiah; it was so with Jeremiah; it was so with Amos. Here it was true of Alma.

The story of the emerging of "the church" among Alma and his people throws light on the process of creating the church. First, Alma lived among the people in a person-with-person way. He met persons "privately." He told his friends about God and about the type of life required for living with God. Next he spoke with them about covenanting with God and with one another. Alma asked the people directly if they wanted to come into "the fold of God" and "to be called the people of God." This term "fold of God" is a significant designation of what the church is to be.

Alma did some first-class ministering in interpreting the function of baptism in the life of the church. It was to be "a witness" of entering into a "covenant" with God (Mosiah 9:41). In this covenant persons would promise to live God's way and God would promise to sustain them by his Spirit. Baptism was much more than an initiation rite.

When Alma asked his followers if they wanted to be baptized, he expected a forthright answer from each person. Their response was spontaneous and refreshing. "They clapped their hands for joy, and exclaimed, This is the desire of our hearts!" (Mosiah 9:42) There were no conventional controls, no priesthood pressures, no ritualistic grooves. The salutation in the baptism of Helam is a classic in Book of Mormon materials (9:44).

"About two hundred and four souls" were "baptized in

the waters of Mormon" (9:47, 48). What a congregation! What a fellowship! This was their simple designation, "And they were called the church of God, or the church of Christ, from that time forward" (Mosiah 9:49).

At once Alma looked to the spiritual development and the spiritual fellowship of his people. "Having authority from God," he "ordained priests." These men were to live among the people and minister to them. There was pastoral assignment, "one priest to every fifty of their number" (verse 51). These priests were of the people. They had no privileges of finance and social standing. They were to "labor with their own hands for their support" (9:57, 59). This is in sharp contrast to the parasitical and wasteful ways of the priests of Noah (Mosiah 7:8, 9).

This young and vigorous church was a fellowship of saints. They planned for mutual support. They had a sense of stewardship. They arranged to provide for needing members. This comment is worthy of note: they were to impart "to one another, both temporally and spiritually, according to their needs and their wants" (Mosiah 9:65).

Always these saints lived in danger. The king was looking for them. He regarded Alma and his followers as rebellious and subversive. He meant to get rid of them. The comment of a modern would apply: "It takes grit and guts to be a real follower of Jesus Christ." This church of Alma's people was a church of the courageous.

Yet this was not an in-group that withdrew to themselves and became concerned with their own security and ease. They were not inbred; they drew others to them. They had enough spiritual vitality to do this. Originally "about two hundred and four" were baptized. When the church fled from the army of Noah there were "about four hundred and fifty souls" (Mosiah 9:73).

Two Church Groups Came Together

Eventually Alma and his people had to get away from the harassment. The story is told in Alma's account, Chapter 11 ff. In the land they called Helam they prospered and the outlook was good. Alma was designated as "their high priest" (Mosiah 11:17). He was considered "the founder of their church" (verse 17). At this time situations developed which necessitated their getting out of the country to protect their freedom and their faith.

The Lamanites had come upon the priests of Noah who had fled. Some working arrangement was effected. While the Lamanites were returning from discovering and capturing these priests, they came upon the land of Helam where the people of Alma were living. Amulon, leader of the priests of Noah, rose to a position of influence. He vented his special dislike against the people of Alma, particularly against Alma himself. He issued an order that they might not cry out to God. He decreed that "whosoever should be found calling upon God should be put to death" (Mosiah 11:58). So the people of Alma prayed in silence. They could hold no meetings. They could not converse about their afflictions.

Then came the deliverance (verse 60 ff.). By night, when a "deep sleep" had come upon the Lamanites, the people of Alma departed into the wilderness. An entire congregation gathered. They traveled for twelve days in the wilderness and then arrived at Zarahemla.

The story of the union is told very simply. This account says, "King Mosiah received them with joy." He caused "that all the people should be gathered together" (Mosiah 11:76, 77). There was no examination of beliefs and of creeds. There were no inquisitions into orthodoxy. They got together in common loyalty to God.

There were several groups now comprising the people of

Mosiah: (1) the Nephite people who had stayed on in their homeland, the original Nephite stock with Mosiah their king. (2) The original Zarahemlites, descendants of Mulok, who had been discovered by King Mosiah and his people when they migrated to get away from the Lamanites (Omni 1:24). By the time Mosiah and his people found them, they had become atheistic and corrupt in language and belief (Omni 1:30, 31). These Zarahemlites and the Nephites became one people with Mosiah their king (Omni 1:19). The Zarahemlites outnumbered the Nephites. (3) The company of Alma and his followers, who fled from Lamanite land to Zarehemla. (4) The people of Limhi who also had fled from the Lamanites. Limhi was the third generation of the Nephites who had returned to the lands they had left when they migrated. The first leader of the group that left Zarahemla was Zeniff (Mosiah 6 ff.). The second generation leader was the profligate King Noah. The leader of the third generation was Limhi who, helped by Ammon, a scout from Zarahemla, effected escape from the Lamanites (Mosiah 10).

It took a very vital church with a dynamic evangelistic outreach to effect social unity and spiritual oneness among these diverse sections. Alma went right to work. King Mosiah was at his right hand. The result was gratifying. "King Limhi was desirous that he might be baptized; and all his people were desirous that they might be baptized also. Therefore Alma went forth into the water, and baptized them." As many as were baptized belonged "to the church of God." The missionary endeavor was extended until it was necessary to arrange for several congregations. "They assembled themselves together in different bodies, being called churches" (Mosiah 11:98). Seven congregations were reported. Yet there was one united church: "Notwithstanding there were many churches they were all one church; yea, even the church of God" (Mosiah 11:100).

Growing Pains in the Church

There was a generation gap. The younger people were called "the rising generation." Today the phrase "the rising-up generation" is used. In those days of King Mosiah and Alma these youths tended to break away from "the traditions of their fathers" (Mosiah 11:105). These youth did not catch the spirit or impact of "the words of King Benjamin." They did not believe what their elders said about "the coming of Christ" (Mosiah 11:106). These were the comments of the recorders: "Their hearts were hardened. They would not be baptized; neither would they join the church. And they were a separate people as to their faith" (verses 106-109). Their influence was heightened by "dissensions among the brethren." So their numbers increased. There was a generation gap, a regeneration gap.

Alma and Mosiah took a constructive approach. Persons would be labored with on matters of moral misbehavior. There was to be no persecution or theological compulsion against members or nonmembers. Some things were to be left between the person and God. But the church was to be affirmative, considerate, and move forward constructively.

In this company of youthful "unbelievers" were Alma, the son of Alma, and the four sons of King Mosiah (verse 159). The elders might have called these and their friends "the lost generation." Alma II, clever and sociable, was described as "a great hinderment to the prosperity of the church of God" (Mosiah 11:161). He was an aggressive dissenter and an effective rebel. The four sons of Mosiah were his accomplices.

It took a jolt to get the attention of Alma II. God asked a direct question. First God said, "Alma, arise and stand forth. Why are you persecuting the church of God?" This was followed by a directive and an affirmation: "This is my church, and I will establish it; and nothing shall overthrow it save it is the transgression of my people" (Mosiah 11:166). Then what God said might be put this way, "Alma, get into the church and make it go!"

Fully Functioning Membership

Alma went to work at once. He did not wait to participate until he was forty. He got right into the life of the church. And his four friends Ammon, Aaron, Omner, and Himni went with him. These four chose to go on a dangerous mission to Lamanite land. One after another they gave up their right to the kingship and Alma came into his own. He was high priest of the church and chief judge of the government (Mosiah 13:63).

Now there was no generation gap. These five young men, so charged with zest, made things happen in the church of God.

Factors in Church Decline

The decade before the advent of Christ saw serious decline in the spiritual condition of the church among the Nephites. Worsening conditions in the country and in the church went together. These were conditions as depicted in III Nephi 3: "Some were lifted up unto pride and boastings, because of their exceedingly great riches." "The people began to be distinguished by ranks, according to their riches, and their chances for learning." "Some were lifted up in pride, and others were exceedingly humble." This was one inclusive explanation: "Satan had great power, unto the stirring up of the people to do all manner of iniquity, and to the puffing them up with pride, tempting them to seek for power, and authority, and the vain things of the world." The commentator adds, "They did not sin ignorantly, for they knew the will of God concerning them; . . . they willfully rebelled against God." The few who dared to stand up and speak forth for God were put out of the way (III Nephi 3:28). The society without spiritual values, without sense of worth of persons, pressured its mood and way of life upon the church. By and large the church gave in. A small core group led by Nephi (III Nephi 3:67) raised a warning voice.

Jesus Led in the Living of the Church

Jesus used the term "church" for the first time when he referred to the sacrament of the bread and wine. This was to be served to "the people of my church" (III Nephi 8:32). This was to be a remembrance, a testimony, a covenant for those who believed, who were baptized. This was to be an expression of fellowship, through eating together. Jesus Christ did not have much to say about the church. He did not discuss organization or outline procedures. He did not formulate any creeds. He lived with his people the fellowship and mission of the church.

Jesus did work out some elementary organization. As in Judah, he selected and ordained men to carry on his work. He gave these men on-the-job training while he was with them. In neither place did he leave his work to just anyone who felt the inclination to do something. He called men by name and commissioned them. The first man he summoned was Nephi, son of Nephi, son of Helaman. The others are named in III Nephi 9:4—Timothy, Jonas, Mathoni, Mathonihah, Kumen, Kumenonhi, Jeremiah, Shemnon, Jonas, Zedekiah, Isaiah. This calling of men continued: "There were other disciples ordained in their stead" (IV Nephi 1:16). There were "elders, priests, and teachers" (Moroni 6:2). These were names familiar to these Nephites with Jewish background.

The church was a fellowship with a mission, centered in and vitalized by Jesus Christ. It prospered in outreach, in spiritual vitality, in happiness.

The Abominable Church

The Book of Mormon speaks often of the "great and abominable church" (I Nephi 3:141). Many have spent their time identifying this abominable church in our day, in other days. The Book of Mormon is more concerned in pointing out what makes such a church abominable than in identifying it by name. Here are some of the distinguishing characteristics of such a church: (1) Concern with external manifestations of riches. (2) Desire for "the praise of the world" (I Nephi 3:144). (3) Opposition to those who speak honestly for God. (4) Discontinuance of the covenantal relationship with God (I Nephi 3:169). The sensuousness and selfishness of it all is caught up in the phrase, "the mother of harlots" (I Nephi 3:234). Such an abominable church was expressed in the concoction worked out by Noah and his priests (Mosiah 7:1-22). Here was a church of pretense, laziness, irresponsibility, and sensuousness.

All of this came into expression "when two hundred and ten years had passed away" after the ministry of Christ (IV Nephi 1:29). Churches sprang up in numbers. Some pretended to believe in Christ, but did not. Some openly denied Christ. Some persecuted those who believed in Christ. Some were too careless or too confused to know what belief in Christ truly meant. Some held to the living Christ.

Considerations for Conversation

1. What word do you select for the designative word to indicate what the church is? Which of the following words best expresses your choice: Organization. Cause. Temple.

Fellowship. Society. People. Which best expresses the view of the Book of Mormon?

2. How did Jesus of Nazareth go about creating his church in Judea and Galilee? How did he go about it in the Land Bountiful? What did he do first? And then?

3. What kind of thing happened in the church when it grew strong? When it became weak? What characterizes a strong, healthy church?

4. What kind of program characterized the church that Alma I initiated? How did he make it a functional fellowship?

5. How did Jesus use sacraments for the spiritual development of his people? (Here sacrament means a rite in which ministrant and recipient function with God for spiritual nurture.) How did he use the Lord's Supper, baptism, confirmation, ordination, blessing of children, administration to the sick?

6. What do you see as the role of the church in the Zionic community described in IV Nephi? What did the church contribute to achieving and maintaining this society? How did this Zionic community go to pieces?

7. What do you see as the function in ministry of the men Jesus called to minister during his visit in Land Bountiful? How did he train these men in and for ministry?

8. What pointers do you discover for youth's participation in the work of the church in the revolt of Alma II and the sons of Mosiah? Did they view the church as "the Establishment"? What did they do when they got into the living of the church?

9. What pointers do you find in the Book of Mormon about the role of "priests" in the church and in society? Pointers about things to avoid and about things to do?

10. What pointers does the Book of Mormon give about wholesome congregational living?

11. From the account of Jesus Christ's ministry in the Western land, what do you see as his redemptive role in living among men? (Cf. II Corinthians 5:17 ff.)

Exploration VIII. The Book Narrates Incidents of Note . . . In this exploration happenings are selected for their vitality and relativity to life. They denote how the book sees man working with God, how man thinks of God.

One factor in Bible appreciation and use has been the stories that are narratable, that readers keep remembering and telling. Some of these are actual happenings; some are parables. For a long while boys and girls and youth and adults will remember how David slew Goliath, how Judas betrayed Jesus for thirty pieces of silver, how Saul of Tarsus saw the light on the road to Damascus. These stories live because they are well told, because they reflect the way human nature is, because they "have a point."

Some have said that the Book of Mormon has no such appealing stories. These persons say there are pages and pages from Isaiah, lists of battles, and much sermonizing but no living stories. Perhaps believers in the Book of Mormon are responsible for much of this attitude. For the most part believers have been interested in "proving" the book in doctrinal terms. They quote from the Bible and from the Book of Mormon. They bring in data from American archaeology. Not often do they get into the book and make it live.

Let us go into the book and live some happenings that have vitality, that picture human nature in living terms.

The Building of the Ship

Every red-blooded person who wants to do something creative and worthful will do well to read this story a few times each year. Nephi, a young man, was told to build a ship. This ship was to be sturdy enough to cross the ocean. He was alone when God gave him the assignment. Some would have said, "Where is the hardware store? Where is the lumberyard? Where is the power saw? Where is the naval architect?" Others would have said, "God, I would be glad to build the ship, but . . ." This three-letter word *but* classifies persons. The work of God is ever held back by this word. Nephi could have said, "But I have no tools." God's reply: "Find some ore and make your tools." He could have said, "But I have no lumber." God's reply: "Get to the woods and find some." He could have said, "But there are my brothers." (These complaining, fault-finding brothers were enough to make him hesitant about taking the assignment.) He could have said, "But I have no plans." God assured him on this point: "Come to the mountain and we shall have a laboratory in drawing up plans." Here is a first-class case of faith and works operating together. When the ship was completed it was no thrown-together vessel; it worked. Here is the story of the courageous and creative faith of Nephi. Persons, families, and congregations will do well to read this aloud, to live it through.

What follows is a collection of selected passages adapted from the story of the building of the ship, as narrated by Nephi (I Nephi 5).

In the Land Bountiful the voice of the Lord came to me, saying, "Arise, and get up into the mountain."

So I arose and went up into the mountain, and cried to the Lord.

In the mount the Lord spoke to me and said, "You shall construct a ship, after the manner which I shall show you, that I may carry your people across the waters."

Then I said to the Lord, "Where shall I go to find ore that I may make tools for constructing this ship?"

And God told me where to find ore, that I might make tools.

I also made bellows out of the skins of beasts, for blowing the fire.

And I smote two stones together that I might make fire.

And the Lord said to me, "I will be your light in the wilderness. I will prepare the way before you, if you will keep my commandments. You shall be led to the promised land, and you shall know that I have led you."

When my brothers saw that I was about to build a ship, they murmured, saying, "Our brother is a fool. He thinks that he can build a ship that will cross the great waters."

They did not believe that I was being instructed by the Lord.

They were happy when I was sorrowful at what they said. They kept on, saying, "We know that you cannot construct a ship, for you lack judgment."

Yet they did not dare to lay their hands upon me, nor touch me, for the Spirit of God was with me. And then they said, "We know of a surety that the Lord is with you." They would have worshiped me, but I would not suffer this. I told them, "I am your brother, even your younger brother."

Then they went to work with me, and we worked together on the timbers.

I built the ship after the manner shown me by God.

Often I, Nephi, would go into the mountain, and pray to the Lord. There the Lord showed me many great things.

After I had finished building the ship, according to the word of the Lord, my brothers looked at it and said that it was good and that the workmanship was exceedingly fine. So they were humble before the Lord.

Then the voice of the Lord came to my father, directing that we should arise and go down to the ship. So on the morrow we prepared all things and took our provisions of fruit and meat and honey in abundance and went to the ship. We took also what other things we had brought, including seeds.

We put forth to sea, and we were driven forth before the wind, toward the promised land.

The Family Camp of King Benjamin

This is an abridged version of the story. The Book of Mormon account gets a little heavy with preaching. First of all, let King Benjamin come alive. His sense of stewardship in kingship needs to be heard today. He worked for the good of his people; he made his own living so he would not be a burden to his countrymen. To relive this story we have to see the tents circled around the temple, see the speaking platform erected for the king. We have to catch the genuine respect the Nephites had for their leader. We watch them making a covenant to live together with God. We see how King Benjamin's message was a message of the social gospel that entailed looking out for others in brotherly spirit. Last of all we follow the families as they go to their homes. This story is presented in solo and chorus arrangement. It should be pictured and then read aloud and lived.

This story, adapted from Mosiah 1:14 ff., might be called "the first family camp" on the Western land. It might be called "the social gospel in action" or "a leader who lived with and lived for." The following things stand out: The king's intent to advise his people about what was taking place to enable them to participate understandingly; the outlining of essentials in living together so the people could make their covenant meaningfully; the enlisting of the people on a voluntarism basis; the practical relationship of believing and doing in social relationships; the wholesomeness of the way of life outlined by King Benjamin; the primary place given to family living, even on festival occasions.

Solo: King Benjamin labored with all the might of his body and the faculty of his soul, with the assistance of the prophets, and he established peace in the land.

Chorus: He was a holy man and he reigned over his people in righteousness. He spoke the word of the Lord with power and authority.

Solo: Benjamin had three sons: Mosiah, Helorum, and Helaman.

Chorus: He taught his sons the language of his fathers, that they might become men of understanding, that they might know the teachings of the prophets.

Solo: King Benjamin waxed old, and he thought it expedient that he should confer the kingdom on one of his sons.

Chorus: He sent a proclamation throughout all the land,

to all the people of Zarahemla, summoning them to gather together.

Solo: And the people came up to the temple with gratitude to the just man who had delivered them from enemies and had been their king.

Chorus: They pitched their tents around the temple, every man according to his family, consisting of his wife, his sons and daughters, and their sons and daughters. All came, from the eldest to the youngest. Each family was separate from every other family.

Solo: Then King Benjamin spoke to them, "I have spent my days in your service, without searching for riches from you.

Chorus: "I have labored with my own hands, so you would not be laden with grievous taxes. I have spent my days in your service. I tell you this, that you may learn that when you are in the service of your fellowmen you are in the service of God."

Solo: And King Benjamin said, "Have no mind to injure one another. Live together peaceably. Render to every man that which is his due.

Chorus: "You will not suffer your children to go hungry or naked. "You will teach your children to walk in the way of truth, to love one another, to serve one another."

Solo: And King Benjamin continued, "Give of your substance to the poor, every man according to what he has. Visit the sick; administer relief, both spiritually and temporally.

Chorus: "Be diligent; do things in wisdom and in order,

Solo:	And the people said, "The Spirit of God has wrought a mighty change in us; we want to do good continually.
Chorus:	"We are willing to enter into a covenant with our God to do his will all the remainder of our days."
Solo:	And King Benjamin said to his people, "Because of the covenant which you have made, you shall be called the children of Christ, his sons and daughters."
Chorus:	King Benjamin took the names of all who had entered into the covenant. All except the little children had taken upon them the name of Christ.
Solo:	The king consecrated his son Mosiah to be king and gave him charge concerning the kingdom.
Chorus:	He dismissed the multitude, and they returned to their homes, every one according to his family.

for it is not requisite that a man should run faster than he has strength."

The Martyrdom of Abinadi

This is the story of a courageous man who stood by his convictions. Abinadi stands high on any list of heroes in the Book of Mormon.

First we reconstruct the setting of his life and his death. Noah was the king of the company of Nephites who had returned to their former lands. He was profligate in many ways. His priests furthered his wickedness and provided him companionship in it. Wine and women were their specialties. When they won a victory over the Lamanites they took credit to themselves and "did boast in their own strength."

Abinadi stood up to these men unflinchingly. He even told the king that unless he repented, his life would be "as a garment in a hot furnace" (Mosiah 7:50). He turned on the priests and accused them of misconduct, of abuse of their own people. Abinadi was sentenced to death, but he did not budge an inch.

It is advisable to meet and appreciate the major characters in this story. King Noah stands out as sensuous and self-centered, afraid to do what his better self indicates once in a while. He is well-decorated; he enjoys the fawning of his courtiers, and they know this. Abinadi speaks for himself. He draws appreciative response from any man of spiritual courage. He is a martyr without self-pity, a prophet who knows God well. Alma's quality is also perceived in the story of his life which follows this incident. In this story (Mosiah 7-9:27) numbers do not count. One strong Alma was worth a hundred weaklings.

> There was a man among the people of King Noah whose name was Abinadi. He went forth among the people to call them to repentance, to warn them.
>
> The people were angry, and sought to take his life. King Noah said, "Who is Abinadi that I and my people should be judged of him? Who is he to raise contention among my people? I will slay him."
>
> After two years Abinadi came among the people in disguise, for the Lord directed him to go again and warn the people. He spoke out threatening warnings, even against King Noah.
>
> King Noah caused that Abinadi should be cast into prison. Then he brought his priests together that they might hold a council concerning Abinadi. The priests said, "Bring him hither, that we may question him."
>
> Abinadi answered them boldly, and withstood all their questions. Then he turned on the priests and said to them, "Why do you pervert the ways of the Lord? You sin and you cause the people to sin. You ought to tremble before God!"

Then King Noah said to the priests, "Away with this fellow! Slay him!" But Abinadi withstood them, and said, "Touch me not! God will smite you, if you do." Abinadi spoke with power and authority from God. "I finish my message. Then it matters not whither I go."

One young man whose name was Alma believed the words of Abinadi. He pleaded with the king to let Abinadi depart in peace. The king was angry and sent his servants after Alma to slay him. But Alma fled and could not be found.

After three days Abinadi was brought again before the king and his priests. The king said to Abinadi, "Unless you recall all the words of evil that you have spoken concerning me and my people, you shall be put to death."

Now Abinadi said to the king and the priests, "I will not recall the words which I have spoken to you concerning this people, for they are true. If you slay me, you shed innocent blood."

King Noah was about to release him, for he feared Abinadi's word. But the priests accused Abinadi, saying, "He has reviled the king!"

The king was again stirred up in anger and delivered Abinadi to the priests. They bound him, scourged him, and burned him, even to death.

As the flames began to scorch Abinadi, he cried out, "As you have done to me, so shall it come to pass with you and your seed. You shall be destroyed by your enemies." In their hearing Abinadi said, "O God, receive my soul!"

He fell, sealing the truth of his words by his death.

Rameumptom

This story appeals to those who can picture what was taking place. And it appeals because, as one man has said,

"We tend to do what they did, even chanting the phrases that might be interpreted, 'Look at us! We're pretty good!' "

This took place among a people called the Zoramites who had withdrawn from the Nephites. The Nephites were concerned lest these Zoramites join the Lamanites and reinforce the enemy of the Nephites. Alma and his associates went to the Zoramites in missionary ministry. They found a type of meeting that surprised and shocked them. It centered around a lofty place for praying, in the center of their synagogue, which "Holy Stand" they called *Rameumptom* (Alma 16:97).

Whoever desired to worship had to stand on the top of the "Holy Stand," stretch forth his hands toward heaven, and cry with a loud voice,

> "Holy, holy, God! We believe that thou art God, and we believe that thou art holy, and that thou wast a spirit, and that thou art a spirit, and that thou wilt be a spirit forever.
>
> "Holy God, we believe that thou hast separated us from our brethren . . . ; we believe that thou hast elected us to be thy holy children. . . . We thank thee . . . that we may not be led away after the foolish traditions of our brethren, which doth bind them down to a belief in Christ, which doth lead their hearts to wander far from thee, our God. And again we thank thee, O God, that we are a chosen and a holy people. Amen."—Alma 16:90-94.
>
> "Every man went forth and offered up the same prayers. The place was called by them Rameumptom, which, being interpreted, is the Holy Stand. . . . And after the people had all offered up thanks after this manner, they returned to their homes, never speaking of their God again until they had assembled themselves together again to the holy stand."—Alma 16:96-99.

The Zoramites said their Rameumptom prayers "with a loud voice," with hands stretched toward heaven. Persons and groups with dramatic sense will want to read these "Holy Stand" portions in the same way.

Moroni's Strategy at Gid

This story took place during the war between the Lamanites and the Nephites. Amalickiah, a Nephite, had planned a revolt against his own government. He escaped to the Lamanites and induced them to come against the Nephites. The rebelling Amalickiah, who had maneuvered to become king of the Lamanites, was killed by Teancum, who stole into the camp of Amalickiah at night (Alma 23:40, 41). Then Ammoron, brother of Amalickiah, was made king of the Lamanites. He hated the Nephites with passion. Ammoron wrote to Moroni, captain of the forces of the Nephites, about exchanging prisoners (see Alma 25:1 ff.). Moroni replied in a letter with angry tone. He said, in effect, "If you do not repent, you will go to hell!" (Alma 25:7). He made strong stipulations about the exchanging of prisoners. Ammoron wrote again with a denunciatory message, "We will wage a war which shall be eternal, either to subjecting the Nephites to our authority, or to their eternal extinction" (Alma 25:22).

It was then that Moroni worked out his strategy. It matches the stratagems of ancient times.

> Moroni caused that a search should be made among his men, that he might find a descendant of Laman among them. They found one whose name was Laman.
> Moroni caused that Laman and a small number of his men should go forth to the guards who were over the Nephites, in the city of Gid. When it was evening Laman went to the guards who were over the Nephites. They saw him coming and they hailed him. Laman said to the

guards, "Fear not. I am a Lamanite. We have escaped from the Nephites while they are asleep. We have taken some of their wine, and brought with us."

The Lamanites received him with joy. "Give us of your wine that we may drink, for we are weary."

But Laman said to the guards, "Let us keep our wine until we go against the Nephites."

This saying only made them more desirous to drink the wine. They said, "Let us take of the wine: by and by we shall receive wine for our rations, which will strengthen us to go against the Nephites."

Laman said to them, "You may do according to your desire." So they took of the wine freely. Its taste was pleasant. The wine was strong, for it was prepared for its strength.

When Laman and his men saw that the guards were drunk and in a deep sleep, they returned to Moroni and reported to him. What had happened was according to his design.

Moroni sent men to the city of Gid, while the Lamanites were in a deep sleep and drunken. The men cast in weapons of war to the prisoners so that all were armed, including women and children who were able to bear weapons. All this was done in profound silence.

The Nephites could have slain the Lamanites, but this was not the desire of Moroni.

When the Lamanites awoke in the morning, they were surrounded by the Nephites without, and the prisoners within were armed. The chief captains of the Nephites demanded the weapons of war of the Lamanites. They cast them at the feet of the Nephites, pleading for mercy.

So Moroni took the Lamanites prisoners of war, and he took possession of the city of Gid.

—Adapted from Alma 25:30 ff.

The Sons of Helaman

This is a story of two thousand young men who, during a time that was crucial for their country, risked their lives on a courageous crusade. This is a story for modern times.

The parents and the grandparents of these youths were Lamanites. They had lived in the land of Ishmael with Lamoni as their king. When Ammon and his brothers, sons of King Mosiah, had come among them as missionaries, these Lamanites had been thoroughly converted to the gospel of peace and brotherhood. They had made a vow that they would never again take up arms "for the shedding of blood." They had vowed this "to God, and also to men" (Alma 14:42-47). In time it was expedient for these converted Lamanites to leave their country for safety, for liberty of faith. Ammon negotiated with the Nephite leaders in Zarahemla and arranged for a section of the country called Jershon to be allotted to these newcomers, now often called "the people of Ammon" (Alma 15:15-29). The Nephites provided military protection for these people of Ammon who had taken the vow never to bear arms again.

In time fierce fighting again broke out between the Lamanites and the Nephites. The people of Ammon were troubled because the Nephites were carrying heavy responsibility and paying a high price in lives in defending them. As the situation worsened these men of Ammon were inclined to take up their weapons to give support to the Nephites (Alma 24:68). Helaman advised them against breaking their oath. In those ancient times a vow was made in the name of God, and breaking a vow was therefore an insult to God. At such a time their young sons assembled who had not made this vow. These could fight without breaking an oath. This is the background of this company of young people who went into battle under the leadership of Helaman as told in chapters 24-26 of Alma.

The people of Ammon, the converted Lamanites, made oath that they would never take up arms against their brothers. But in time there were many sons who had not entered into this covenant that they would not take up weapons of war. These entered into a covenant that they would fight for the liberty of the Nephites, that they would lay down their lives to protect the land. There were two thousand young men who made this covenant.

They were all young men, exceedingly valiant for courage, and also for strength and activity; but this was not all: they were men who were true at all times in whatever thing they were entrusted. Yea, they were men of truth and soberness, for they had been taught to keep the commandments of God, and to walk uprightly before him.

Helaman marched at the head of his two thousand stripling soldiers, to the support of the people on the borders of the land on the south by the west sea. They saw the Lamanites and for a while they pursued the Lamanites. Then said Helaman, "My sons, will you go against them to battle?"

And the youth said to Helaman, "Father, our God is with us, and he will not suffer us to fall; then let us go forth!"

These youth thought more of the liberty of their fathers than they did of their lives. They had been taught by their mothers that if they did not doubt, God would deliver them. They rehearsed to Helaman the words of their mothers, saying, "We do not doubt our mothers knew."

After the fighting, Helaman numbered his young men, and he reported, "To my great joy, not one of them had fallen to the earth; they had fought as with the strength of God."

Later the Lamanites fell upon the Nephites again.

The sons of Helaman fought desperately and stood firm. When others of the Nephites were about to give way before the Lamanites, these two thousand and sixty sons were undaunted; they performed every word of command with exactness.

According to the goodness of God, to our great astonishment, to the joy of the whole army, not one soul among these sons of Helaman had perished. Such was the faith of these two thousand youth. Their minds were firm; they put their trust in God continually.

The Other Sheep

Jesus Christ was concluding his "Sermon on the Mount" in Land Bountiful. He turned in memory to what he had been doing in the Jerusalem country. He told his people of the Western land how he had endeavored to tell his fellow Jews over there about some "other sheep" whom he was going to visit. The Jews did not understand. He credited this to their "stiff-neckedness and unbelief" (III Nephi 7:17). Now he was able to tell these Nephites that they were the "other sheep" whom he had had in mind. Then he moved on to one of his memorable teachings. He made his mission truly worldwide. Now as then there are many who do not accept the message. Maybe there is today some "stiff-neckedness and unbelief." Let these words ring out:

"I have other sheep, which are not of this land; neither of the land of Jerusalem; neither in any parts of that land round about where I have been to minister. . . . Neither have I manifested myself unto them. . . . I shall go to them . . . that there may be one fold and one shepherd."—III Nephi 7:24-26.

This happening in Land Bountiful is being lived in many places today. On Christmas Day 1968 William E. Connell and his companion Ruby were in the Choolaimede congregation.

He told them of the "other sheep" of the Good Shepherd. He spoke in English, which was translated into Tamil. A few weeks later he was meeting with "the sheep" in Orissa with the ones who lived inland. It took a jungle journey to get there. This time W. W. Chawla translated his message into the language of Orissa and a second interpreter put this translation into the local language of the Soras. Three languages for one fold. One faith. One fraternity. Most of all, one Shepherd.

Today let every person, every family, every congregation relive what happened that day in Land Bountiful when the one Shepherd spoke of his "other sheep," when he spoke of "one fold." Then let each one live this today with "other sheep" in other lands and in one's own city. And let all hear and heed the Good Shepherd!

Considerations for Conversation

1. How do we reconstruct a situation so we really "live it" and do more than repeat words? How do we go about "walking in the moccasins of the other Indian"?

2. How may believers in the Book of Mormon be so intent to "prove" it that they have fallen short in "living it"?

3. What is there in the story of the building of the ship by Nephi that makes it a top-ranking story? Picture it in terms of some project God could assign a youth in modern times. What are some "but's" the youth might think of? What are some obstacles? For what would the youth go to the mount? Might it be a team project?

4. The family camp of King Benjamin was a "project with purpose." What made it so? What would make a family camp or a family reunion a "project with purpose" today?

5. What qualifies Abinadi for a place on the roster of great martyrs? How might a person have a role today that might not involve physical death but would call for heroic

stuff? What is the difference between surrender of value and conference in voice? What constitutes spiritual courage?

6. What was there in the Rameumptom situation that tends to recur throughout history? What was the outlook of the Zoramites? How may persons be excluded from churches and congregations today?

7. How might "the sons of Helaman" be said to bring together spiritual integrity and fearless faith? What was the relationship between the youths and their leader? How was this relationship highly significant? What quality of faith did these young men express?

8. How did the Jew-Gentile situation complicate the picture of the "other sheep"? What are some "other sheep" that complicate the picture for us today? Do we prefer to keep them in "other pens"?

9. Relive the story of Nephi and his broken bow, as told in I Nephi 5. Note the connecting directive, "By small means, the Lord can bring about great things" (I Nephi 5:36). Tell this story in terms of a youth living today, with whatever his broken bow might be.

Exploration IX. The Book Pictures Persons Worth Knowing . . . Worthy writing depicts persons as humans in the business of living. Meritorious writing conveys insight into human nature. The book pictures those who get with God and those who get away from God.

The centuries have rated William Shakespeare as an artist in portraying persons. The persons he pictured live everywhere. Names and conditions may change but the basic qualities can be observed and identified. He portrayed how persons struggled with problems and the results of the struggles. He brought persons on stage to live with others, to be liked or disliked. Everywhere we see a Hamlet struggling in chronic indecision, and so complex that we can hardly get hold of his tensions. Everywhere we see a Macbeth fired with inordinate ambition until his principles fall by the way. Everywhere we see a Shylock with shekel motivation encouraged by the social uncertainty in which he finds himself. The list might go on and on. Shakespeare stands as one of literature's greats for his portrayal of humans.

The Bible Is Rated High

Once William Lyon Phelps wrote that the Bible is a masterpiece in the portrayal of persons. The men and women of the Bible were in the business of living. The characters are more than anemic symbols, more than robots, more than de-earthed saints. There is a variety of saints and devils, of the lazy and the energetic, of the limited and the gifted, of the parasites and the contributors. There are both in-this-world persons and out-of-this-world persons. Names out of the Bible have come to denote certain character types. We know what a person means when he calls someone a Judas, a Zaccheus, or an Elihu.

And Jesus himself appreciated all this. Sometimes we wonder if he was deliberate in choosing such a variety of men for his Twelve. No two were alike. Here was Nathaniel, whom Jesus rated as "an Israelite in whom was no guile"; the opposite was Judas Iscariot whose motivations dropped pretty low. Here was Matthew who had been a tax collector for the Roman government and opposite was Simon Zealotes who would get rid of the Romans by force. Here was James, called "the Silent," and nearby was Simon Peter who ever seemed to have something to say. It is not unlikely that these several men got on each other's nerves. Probably they "told each other off." Therein lies the artistry of the Bible.

What of the Book of Mormon?

Let us get inside the Book of Mormon and see if there are any persons who stand out clearly, distinctly. This exploration assumes that there are persons worth meeting. Once again let it be said that the believers in the book may have been so busy "proving" it that they have never really lived in it and become acquainted with its characters.

There are some things about the book which have some bearing on its delineation of characters: (1) It is described as coming to be as it is through redacting and abridging. This summarizing tends to eliminate the vivid portrayal of people.

(2) Quotations from Hebrew scriptures present the doctrinal and prophetic sections rather than those parts that picture persons in the business of living. (3) The preoccupation of the writers with records and record-keeping has a bearing. The listings and the genealogies do not speak with vitality. (The twenty-sixth chapter of I Chronicles exemplifies this.) The attention to wars, with the focus on battles, strategies, and chiefs, does not encourage outstanding portrayal of persons. Nevertheless, there are vital persons in the Book of Mormon who compare with those in the Bible. Let's meet them!

Persons Are What Matters

Through the Book of Mormon runs the theology that in God's planning and processing, man as person is foremost; all else is secondary. And there is to be an eternal quality in man as person, so that he is capable of living on and on. There is also the theology that everything exists in relationships—that man, too, has to learn how to live in right relationships with God, with other men, with what is in God's universe. The prophets of vision in the Book of Mormon would say with Gerald Kennedy, "The Christian view of life is based on belief that persons are worth more than anything else."

Yet the book is honest in recognizing that many men do not get on the Way or do not stay on the Way. They get out of touch in differing degrees. There are those in the book who might be mentioned as artists in living. There are others who might line up with Christopher Morley's identification of a human being as "an ingenious assembly of portable plumbing." The book is honest and inclusive.

A Company of Foremost Persons in the Book

Here is a roster of men who stand to the fore. There is no

inclination to rule out the women. Women never got into the book to any degree. This record reflects Hebrew priority for men. Only three women are named in the book, and they do not upgrade the standing of women: (1) Sariah, the wife of Lehi, did not seem sure what their project was all about. She had a gift for complaining. (2) Abish was a working woman in the court of King Lamoni, immature in her faith but willing to do as she saw things that should be done. (3) Isabel, designated as a "harlot," specialized in leading men astray. So our roster will be composed of men. They are worth knowing. They dared to be themselves.

1. Nephi ben Lehi, pioneer builder and colony director.
2. Benjamin, the "good king" who led his people in building a good society.
3. Noah, the renegade king, who undermined and oppressed his people.
4. Abinadi, courageous martyr for his faith.
5. Alma ben Alma, religious reformer and revivalist.
6. Ammon ben Mosiah, the ex-prime missionary to the Lamanites.
7. Moroni, captain of the forces for liberty and faith in God.
8. Mormon, last general of the Nephites, redactor of their records.

These men can come right out on the stage of life and be recognized, with each "in his own style." They are not duplicates. They come alive as we let them.

A Company of Men to Be Recognized

The sixteen men in the list which follows played a significant role in the story in the book. Some run into the general story without much identification. Such are Jared and Ether and Mulok. Some stand out clearly with distinctives which identify them. Such are Lamoni and Korihor and Samuel the Lamanite. What an assembly they would make if they were to come together!

1. Jared, the leader of the first expedition in the eight barges.
2. Jared's brother, spiritual leader of the first colony, the man whose name is not given in the record.
3. Ether, the last prophet of the Jaredites, after whom their record is named.
4. Coriantumr, the lone survivor of the Jaredites, discovered by the Mulokites, of Zarahemla (see Omni 1:35-39).
5. Lehi, the initiator of the migration from Jerusalem and founder of the Nephite colony.
6. Laman, oldest son of Lehi, the leader of the rebellious protest group and founder of the Lamanites.
7. Mulok, the leader of the colony that came out of Jerusalem just after the Nephite group left.
8. Limhi, the leader of a Nephite group that returned to Lamanite land, who led the colony back to Zarahemla.
9. Lamoni, a king of the Lamanites who was converted to Christian faith through the ministry of Ammon.
10. Korihor, sign-seeking agnostic.
11. Amalickiah, Nephite rebel, dissenter to the Lamanites.
12. Helaman, Nephite leader of the two thousand youth of the people of Ammon.
13. Gadianton, leader of the robber bands that harassed the Nephites.
14. Samuel, the Lamanite prophet who warned the people of Zarahemla.
15. Nephi ben Nephi, first apostle chosen by Jesus Christ in Land Bountiful.
16. Moroni, son of Mormon, the last Nephite.

Our Selection of Three Great Nephites

Now we are going to meet two outstanding men. In our limited time we may not come to know scores of persons. We can have superficial contact with many persons, yet never come to know any of them. We would like to meet these two on the level of friendship which says, "A friend is a fellow who sees me as I am and loves me anyway." There will be no hundred percent models in our companies. We shall try to see honestly.

Nephi, the Pioneer Builder

Nephi was a big man in more ways than one. He said of himself, "I, Nephi, being a man large in stature, and also having received much strength of the Lord" (I Nephi 1:135). It took a man of good spiritual and physical dimensions and vitality to do what he did. He was a man to challenge admiration, yet this admiration has tended to exclude examination. In fairness, we need to see the whole Nephi, not to run him down but to appreciate him soundly.

Nephi expressed gratitude for his parents, for his upbringing. The opening sentence of the book says, "I, Nephi, having been born of goodly parents, was taught somewhat in all the learning of my father." Some have wondered at the significance of this word "somewhat." And some have looked at "the learning of my father." It appears that he and his father Lehi had much in common and spent much time together. Did this make him papa's pet in the eyes of his brothers? Did they resent the fact that a younger son had greater access to their father than they did? These older sons considered their father a "visionary man," an impractical dreamer, who was leading them on a wild goose chase.

The material of the first books of the Book of Mormon points to the Eastern culture. There is no shrinking from using the first-person pronoun. Readily did Nephi report, "The Lord spoke to me, saying, 'Blessed art thou, Nephi, because of thy faith, for thou hast sought me diligently, with lowliness of heart' " (I Nephi 1:53). This was the mood of the East. The style does not express self-centeredness as much as inner confidence. Nephi's life was built on the conviction that God was with him, that God had something for him to do.

Nephi was the son commissioned to go back to Jerusalem to procure the Jewish writings that Lehi wanted. It appears that he was the one son who had the courage to take the risk. The slogan of his life is expressed in what he said to his father.

"I will go and do the things which the Lord has commanded, for I know that the Lord gives no commandments to the children of men save he shall prepare a way for them that they may accomplish the thing which he commands them."—I Nephi 1:65.

So the brothers started on their mission. The older brothers, Laman and Lemuel, were filled with distrust and dislike for Nephi. It hardly helped when they were told, "Know you not that the Lord has chosen him to be a ruler over you, and this because of your iniquities?"

It was Nephi who managed to get the writings, the brass plates. His courageous faith and his get-into-action policy brought the sons and the records to Lehi.

Nephi was the foremost hunter in providing food for the families as they moved into the wilderness. When he broke his bow, his brothers censured him for the accident, and no food was obtained for the camp. When he had constructed a new bow and had gone to areas to which he was directed, Nephi came home with ample food. This was his simple statement about the response of the brothers, "When they beheld that I had obtained food, how great was their joy"

(I Nephi 5:40). The story indicates that the brothers liked his contribution of food but resented his competency.

The story of the building of the ship brings to the fore the strength and resourcefulness of Nephi. No tools. No lumber. No architect's plans. No encouragement from his brothers. Yet Nephi built a ship. He clung to the word of promise, "I will be your light in the wilderness" (I Nephi 5:77). All the while his brothers were making caustic comments like "Our brother is a fool, for he thinks that he can build a ship; and he also thinks that he can cross these great waters" (I Nephi 5:86, 87). But Nephi kept going; he hammered at boards and he hammered at his brothers.

Then came the voyage across the ocean. What a nightmare. The older brothers went after Nephi with "rudeness" and with "harshness" and bound him with cords. Lehi seemed unable to hold things together. A threatening storm jarred the rebellious brothers into releasing their younger brother.

Then came the landing apparently in tropical country. Grain culture and animal culture began at once. Nephi took up the task of providing plates and making a record of the colony. This record was generously sprinkled with preaching to his brothers, who were disinclined to lean very strongly toward faith in God. There were rumblings in the family. There were dangers of revolt. But the colony progressed materially. Nephi was a worker and a manager.

Then came the deciding and dividing event: Lehi died (II Nephi 3:23). Laman and Lemuel turned against Nephi, threatening his life. They said defiantly, "We will not have him to be our ruler; for it belongs to us, who are the elder brethren, to rule over this people." There was no resolution of the long-standing hostility.

So Nephi and his three younger brothers and sisters fled

into the wilderness and journeyed "for the space of many days" (II Nephi 4:10). They effected a new settlement which they called Nephi. Here Nephi had his first opportunity to build the kind of community which he had envisioned in his dreams. They "began to prosper exceedingly" (verse 15). They built a temple. Nephi commented, "It came to pass that we lived after the manner of happiness" (II Nephi 4:43).

Nephi was the key figure. He procured the records. He built the ship. He guided the course to "the land of promise." He was the hunter who provided food. He was the keeper of records. He was the provider of Jewish scriptures. He was the director of grain and animal culture. He maintained morale. He was the priest and the teacher. he was the prophet of the coming of Christ. He was the Hebrew who saw what God intended their mission to be. He was a poet: his hymn of rejoicing is a message of beauty. He trained his brothers to be able to carry on after him. He carried the welfare of his people on his heart, his mind. In his later years it was recorded that "The people loved Nephi exceedingly" (Jacob 1:10).

This was the simple closing sentence about his life: "It came to pass that Nephi died" (Jacob 1:12). Yet he lived on in Nephite history.

Ammon, Missionary to the Lamanites

Ammon ranks with the truly great men of missionary story. He had no time for pink-tea religion and "comfortable" prayer meetings; his God was not sitting on padded cushions in a throne chair.

The four princes of Mosiah—Ammon, Aaron, Omner, and Himni—did an about-face when Alma was converted. They had been in the cynical, faith-destroying group. At once they wanted a man-size job. They gave up their right to the throne. They asked permission of their father to "go up to the land of Nephi," to the Lamanites (Mosiah 12:1 ff.). The father king "inquired of the Lord." The answer came back, "Let them go!" The next fourteen years constitute a great story of frontier faith.

These four sons and their associates had no passage provided. "They departed out of the land of Zarahemla, and took their swords, and their spears, and their bows, and their arrows, and their slings. And this they did that they might provide food for themselves while in the wilderness" (Alma 12:11, 12). "They journeyed many days in the wilderness." As they traveled, this assurance came as God's directive: "Go forth among the Lamanites, thy brethren. . . . I will make an instrument of thee in my hands to the salvation of many souls" (Alma 12:18, 19).

At the border of Lamanite land, the four brothers went in different directions. Ammon went into the land of Ishmael. At once "the Lamanites took him and bound him" and carried him to their king, Lamoni. The king asked Ammon if he intended to live among them. Ammon answered wisely, "Yes, I desire to dwell among this people for a time, perhaps until the day I die" (Alma 12:33 ff.). Ammon must have made a most favorable impression, for the king offered to make him his son-in-law. Ammon replied, "No, but I will be your servant."

Ammon was assigned to be a herdsman, and a top-notch herdsman he was. When rustlers raided the king's flocks, Ammon went after them and brought back the king's sheep. This made a tremendous impression on the shepherds and the king. They concluded that "Surely, this is more than a man" (Alma 12:63). King Lamoni observed, "There has not been any servant among all my servants that has been so faithful as this man" (Alma 12:80). When Ammon stood before the king, the king was silent "for the space of an hour, according to their time" (Alma 12:86). Ammon perceived that the king was wondering if he, Ammon, was the Great Spirit. Ammon said in response, "I am a man and am your servant; therefore, whatever thou desirest which is right, that will I do" (Alma 12:91). There was willingness to work but indisposition to compromise his values. He explained his ability to perceive what the king was thinking in this way: "I am called by [the] Holy Spirit to teach these things to this people. . . . And a portion of that Spirit dwelleth in me."

The collapse of the king, the response of the queen, the news-carrying of Abish make up a moving testimony. Some of the people looked at Ammon with suspicion when the king sank down. Was not this man a Nephite? When King Lamoni regained his composure he stood before the people and recounted his conversion. He and the people of the court said "the selfsame thing: that their hearts had been changed, that they had no more desire to do evil" (Alma 12:176). Lamoni and Ammon became brothers in faith, with deep spiritual affection.

The spiritual genius of Ammon rises to its heights in his testimonial recounting to his brothers of what had happened during their fourteen years among the Lamanites. It is one of the most fervent outpourings of evangelistic spirit in all scripture. Ammon was so enthusiastic that his brother Aaron accused him of boasting (Alma 14:90). Ammon spoke out of the overflow of his heart and said, "I will not boast of myself; I will boast of God. If this be boasting, then let me boast!" He recalled how their own Nephites reacted when the four young men had said that they were going to go to the Lamanites: "they laughed us to scorn." Then he went on to say, "We have been instruments in the hands of God, to bring about this great work." What these men had done had carried them into danger after danger. This was the summary statement of Ammon to his brothers:

"We have entered into their houses and taught them, and we have taught them in their streets, upon their hills, in their temples and synagogues. We have been cast out, and mocked, and spit upon; we have been smitten upon our cheeks; we have been stoned, bound with cords, and cast into prison. Through the power and wisdom of God we have been delivered. We have suffered all manner of afflictions, that we might be the means of saving some soul."

Ammon's gospel involved more than mouthing words. He sensed the dangers for these Lamanites who had been converted. Their countrymen would go against them. So he engineered the project of moving these people up to the land of Zarahemla where the Nephites granted them the land of Jershon for their own settlement. Ammon was wise enough to present the matter to the Nephites and procure their assenting voice before he brought these Lamanites in to live. Henceforth the Nephites called these migrants "the people of Ammon." This was a fitting tribute to a wise and fervent missionary.

Another reward for Ammon lay in what happened in the lives of these people. They renounced war and buried their arms. "They were distinguished for their zeal towards God, and also towards men. They were honest and upright in all things. They were firm in the faith of Christ."

Then Ammon went to work ministering among the Nephites. There emerged a wonderful period in Nephite history. There was "continual peace" and "exceedingly great prosperity in the church." This was possible through the work of ministers of merit, among them Ammon (Alma 21:185).

A man like Ammon never quits his spiritual adventure.

The Main Character—Jesus Christ

The Book of Mormon was "to come forth by the gift and power of God . . . to the convincing of the Jew and Gentile that Jesus is the Christ, the Eternal God, manifesting himself unto all nations." The two words that stand out are "convincing" and "manifesting." Unfortunately we have associated "convincing" with arguing and proving a point. Often we need to see that convincing can come through seeing in action. An old fellow had seen pictures of giraffes and had read descriptions of them. They looked too impossible for him. Then one day he went to the zoo and saw the long-necked quadruped for himself. He could only admit, "There it is." This is the way of the Book of Mormon with Jesus Christ.

Read the story of Christ himself in III Nephi. He is moving about among men and women, boys and girls. He is conversing with them. He is praying with them. He is administering bread and wine in covenanting fellowship. He is ministering to their sick and making them whole. The upshot of it all is that the Son of God is living with the sons of men as friend, as father. And something tremendous is happening in these persons. They are being reborn with newness of life. This Christ was not frightening them or overawing them. He was not holding them to him with signs and wonders. He was generous in pouring out his life to them. And they were ever wanting more.

The Book of Mormon portrays the friendly, caring, lifting, inspiring Christ. And it keeps saying to us today, "Hear him!"

Considerations for Conversation

1. How do scriptures of merit picture man (a) as he is on his own and (b) as he is when he gets with God? What

constitutes an unhealthy way of getting with God and a healthy way of getting with God?

2. How is it meritorious for the Book of Mormon to picture characters like Noah and Korihor as well as characters like Ammon and Captain Moroni?

3. How is it desirable to see the overall picture of the family of Lehi in operation so that we get the viewpoints and reactions of Laman as well as those of Nephi? How did Lehi and Sariah function in the family? Do you see any way of getting Laman and Lemuel into the corporate spirit of the family? What qualities made Nephi a man of rugged spirituality?

4. What do you find superficial in the views and sayings of Korihor? (See Alma 16:13 ff.). Do you see him interested in obtaining information or in dialoguing? How may the question asked in Alma 16:48 be considered a legitimate question? What kind of sign did Korihor want?

5. What qualities and abilities stand out in Ammon in the story of his going to the Lamanites, in his meeting with King Lamoni? (See Alma 12.) What did he do and what did he say that express greatness? How did he converse with King Lamoni with appreciation of King Lamoni's background? How might Ammon be called a "great missionary"?

6. How might the motivation for keeping the records of the Nephites and the method of abridging affect the human interest and portrayal of the book? What materials did the recorders aim to include in the record?

7. How might the story of Ammon be entitled, "How God Works in the Life of a Man"? How do you see God at work in the life of Ammon?

8. How is the evaluation of Captain Moroni given in Alma 21:132-134 a significant estimation of this unusual man? What in Moroni makes him stand out as a man of stalwart spirituality?

9. How did the Twelve chosen by Jesus in Judea and in Galilee constitute an unusual diversity of persons? How did some differ? Do you think that this was intentional? Do you suppose that Jesus Christ had such a range of personhood in the company of men named in III Nephi 9:4?

10. There is a saying that we tend to close our eyes to the weaknesses of our heroes and see only their strengths. What are some things in the lives of Nephi ben Lehi, Ammon ben Mosiah, and Alma ben Alma that express the less heroic?

11. What would you see Nephi ben Lehi, Ammon ben Mosiah, and Captain Moroni doing today that would make them heroic in current living?

12. How does the Book of Mormon tell the story of Jesus Christ's visit to the Western land so that he lives among people in an uplifting association that rises above the way of signs and wonders? How did he get near to the people while he was near to his Father?

Exploration X. The Book Contains Passages of Merit . . . Scriptures of good quality are quotable. They say something of worth in appealing manner. Here foremost passages are presented in literary format, for fidelity to their own nature.

On the whole the Book of Mormon has seldom been explored for passages of merit. It has been used to support a point of doctrine or to sustain its place as scripture. This exploration sets out to locate passages of vitality and beauty. Let these speak in their own right.

Enduring Writings Are Quotable

We say with Shakespeare, "To be or not to be—that is the question," because persons are ever feeling this way and asking this way. We say with Abraham Lincoln, "With malice toward none, with charity toward all," for the contrast persists. We say with the sages of the book of Proverbs, "Where there is no vision, the people perish," because this ever holds true, and because it is so pithily stated. We say with Jesus of Nazareth, "Where your treasure is, there will your heart be also." Is there anything like this in the Book of Mormon?

In works of literary and spiritual merit, a section, some

sentence, or even a phrase may be singled out. Passages of merit and appeal are quoted over and over. Scriptures that are not quoted are soon forgotten.

The Bible Has Well Known Sections

The Bible has been the world's most quoted book. It has passages and sayings that are classic. This applies to content and to literary expression. These passages were never selected by any voting parliament of religion. Use and appreciation of them by many types of persons have brought them into prominence. Some parts of the Bible are scarcely fingered — the listing of names, as in the second chapter of Ezra; the genealogy in the opening chapters of the book of Matthew. There are other pages that are soiled and worn from use. Readers are selective.

The Bible has passages that are known and used around the world. Mahatma Gandhi often read the passages about the love of Jesus of Nazareth that prompted him to give everything he had for mankind. A Jewish rabbi chose to read again and again what Paul wrote about the indispensability of love. A roll call of a group of Latter Day Saints would bring out loved portions that would make a roster of quotable passages and sayings. There are quotations that stand out for all time. Such is the Golden Rule, "Whatsoever you would that men should do to you, do you even so to them" (Matthew 7:21).

Does the Book of Mormon Have Such Passages?

In this exploration some choice passages are presented. They will be printed in format conducive to reading, suitable to the nature of the passage. On the whole the Book of Mormon does not make reading easy. The division into chapters and verses is not helpful. The producers of the book did not give attention to this detail. Sometimes the Bible has met the same fate. Here a format suited to the nature of the passage will be used.

Here again let the book speak for itself. When it speaks we shall endeavor to reconstruct the setting and the purpose. We shall live with an Alma or an Ammon as we would an Isaiah, a Paul of Tarsus, a Benjamin Franklin, or a Robert Browning. Of this we can be certain: if the passage has merit, it will continue to speak. It will become part of the world's library of scriptures.

Soliloquy on Evangelistic Ministry

Alma is speaking out of a troubled situation. A disastrous war between the Nephites and the Lamanites has just come to a close. Casualties have been heavy. Anguish of mourning pervades the country. Alma is saying to himself, "Must there be war? Is there not a better way?" As he wonders, he sees two things in contrast: "sorrow because of death and destruction among men, and joy because of the light of Christ unto life" (Alma 15:51). The longing to be a missionary with the gospel of transforming spiritual power prompts Alma to pour out his soul in reflection. There is nothing in scripture that stands above it. It rises to the height when he senses the satisfaction of affecting one life for good. Here is an affirmation of the worth of every person. Here is the expression of true evangelistic joy. There is no concern for rewards for "conversions." Here is expressed the satisfaction of finding brotherly consociation in Christ (see Doctrine and Covenants 16:2c-d).

What is given here is an abridged version of selected passages. The group should read this aloud and read again in silence.

O that I were an angel
and could have the wish of my heart,
that I might go forth
and speak with the trump of God,
with a voice to shake the earth,
and cry repentance to this people!

Yea, I would declare unto every soul,
as with the voice of thunder,
repentance and the plan of salvation,
that they might repent, and come unto our God,
that there might be no more sorrow
upon all the face of the earth.

But behold, I am a man,
And I do sin in my wish!
I ought to be content
with the things which the Lord
has allotted to me.

I know that he allots unto men
according to their wills,
whether they be to salvation
or unto destruction.

Now, seeing these things,
why should I desire more
than to perform this work to which I have been called?

Why should I wish that I were an angel,
that I could speak
unto all the ends of the earth?
I know that the Lord has commanded me,
and I glory in it,
not of myself, but in the Lord.

And this is my glory,
that perhaps I may be an instrument
in the hands of God
to bring some soul to repentance.

And this is my joy!

Prophecy Concerning the Land of Promise

The selection which follows comes from the farewell
message of Lehi, just before his death. He had brought his
sons and their families to the Western land with a sense of
mission. This new country was to have a significant role in
God's ongoing purpose. Here Lehi speaks of the stewardship
of living in this "goodly land." He makes continuity and
prosperity contingent upon the way the people live in their
new "land of promise."

Lehi looks to the future of the land after his time. He
sees the opening of the land to Gentile occupation and
settlement as this fits into God's program.

What is said here about "the land of promise" applies to
the living of peoples on any continent. It certainly applies to
America in these times. Key words are "righteousness" and
"liberty"; he makes the two go together. He reminds his sons
that these things do not come by chance; only a people active
in goodness can achieve and maintain freedom and right. The
selected portions come from the first chapter of II Nephi.
Lehi's words should ring out in modern times.

We have obtained a land of promise,
a land which is choice above all lands,
a land covenanted to me and to my children.

It shall be a land of promise
    to all those who shall be led
        out of other countries
    by the hand of the Lord.

So this land is consecrated unto those
    whom the Lord shall bring.

If those who come shall serve him,
    according to the commandments
        which he has given them,
    it shall be a land of liberty unto them.

If they shall ever be brought down,
    it shall be because of their iniquity.

Unto the righteous,
    this land shall be blessed forever.

It is wisdom that this land shall be kept yet
    from the knowledge of other nations;
    for many nations would overrun the land,
    so there would be no place for an inheritance.

If those who dwell in this land shall dwindle in unbelief,
    after they have received
        so great blessings from the Lord,
    after they have been brought
        by the infinite goodness of God
    unto this precious land of promise,
    then the Lord will bring other nations,
    and these shall have power,
    while our people shall be scattered and smitten.

O my sons, may not these judgments come upon you!
    May you be a choice and favored people of the Lord!

Arise from the dust, my sons and be men,
    and be determined in one mind,
    and be united in one heart in all things,
    that you may prosper in this land.

Let this be to you and to your children
    a land of promise,
    a land of righteousness.

The Functioning of Faith

The classic adapted for use here is rightly called a treatise, a testimony, on "the functioning of faith." Here Alma interprets faith as a growing experience, ever in process. Faith does not come all at once and does not "stay put" as a finished product. Alma likens faith experience to the growing of a fruit-bearing tree from a simple seed. He uses the words "experiment" and "exercise." Faith-nurturing and fruit-bearing go together. And such a faith has roots; it is more than wishing and daydreaming. Planting and cultivating are involved.

Alma had just been among the Zoramites. He had noted their strange Rameumptom form of worship (see Alma 16:97 ff.). This required little of the worshipers and brought forth little from them. It caused a breach between the well-to-do and the less privileged and identified divine favor with material things. Against this background Alma poured out his reflections on dynamic, exacting, adventuring faith. He made faith operative in the laboratory of living.

This is a digest of his longer treatise. It brings together his key comments. The material begins with Alma 16:139.

If you have faith,
you hope for things which are not seen,
which are true.

There are many who say,
If you will show us a sign from heaven,
then we will know of a surety;
then we shall believe.

Now I ask you, Is this faith?
I say unto you that it is not.
Faith is hope for things not yet seen,
things which are true.

And this is so with my words.
Awake and arouse your faculties
and experiment upon my words.
Exercise a particle of faith.

Compare the word unto a seed.
If a seed is planted in your heart,
        a true seed, a good seed,
if you do not cast it out by your unbelief,
if you resist not the Spirit of the Lord,
it will begin to swell within you.

You will say to yourself,
This must be a good seed,
for it begins to enlighten my understanding.

Because you have tried the experiment,
when you planted the seed,
and because it swells, and sprouts and grows,
you will know that the seed is good.

As the seed grows into a tree, you will say,
Let us nourish the tree, with great care,
that it may grow and bring forth fruit.

The seed may be good, but your ground may be barren,
and you may not nourish the tree,
so you will not have fruit from it.

When I speak to you,
you do not know of the surety
of my words at first:
you must experiment upon them.

If you will nourish the seed that is planted,
and nourish the tree,
there will be a tree springing up into everlasting life.

Counsel About Praying

This is an abridgment of a sermon that Amulek preached upon Hill Onidah in the land of the Zoramites (Alma 16:124). His congregation was composed for the most part of the poor people who had been excluded from the synagogue. They had lamented that they had been kept from entering the building. Alma had said to them quite directly, "Do you suppose that you can worship God only in your synagogue?" (Alma 16:130). It was then that Alma gave his message about faith which pertained to living everywhere, all the time. He had given faith a dynamic turn. Then Amulek "arose and began to teach them." He gave praying the same functioning quality that Alma had given faith. Praying was not escaping, not leaving things up to God. Praying was interpreted as conversing with God about what we are doing with Him.

The meeting of Alma and Amulek makes a story worth narrating (see Alma 6:23 ff.). Alma was weary and hungry when he came to the city of Ammonihah. He met a stranger and asked him for "something to eat." The stranger was Amulek. This man, of hospitable spirit, took Alma to his home and provided for his food and rest. Alma was instructed by God to call Amulek to be his fellow minister. Later Amulek told how he had been prompted by this unusual warning, "Amulek, return to your house, for you shall feed . . . a chosen man of God" (Alma 8:10). Amulek spoke of himself as "a man of no small reputation, with many kindred and friends," with "much riches" that he had acquired through his own "industry" (verse 5).

This message on prayer is of value for its inclusive and pragmatic application. Here praying is getting with God, talking with God, working with God. Here working and praying are inseparably connected. Amulek could talk with God, for he was doing something with God.

> May God grant you, my brothers,
> that you may begin to exercise your faith
> unto repentance,
> that you may begin to call upon his holy name.
>
> Cry unto him when you are in your fields;
> yea, cry over all your flocks.
> Cry unto him in your houses, over your households,
> morning, midday, and evening.
>
> When you do cry unto the Lord,
> let your hearts be full, drawn out in prayer,
> unto him, continually,
> for your welfare,
> for the welfare of those who are about you.

Do not suppose that this is all:
For after you have done all these things,
if you turn away the needy, and the naked,
and visit not the sick and the afflicted,
and impart not of your substance, if you have,
to those who stand in need,
your prayer is vain and avails you nothing.

Watch that you pray continually.

Psalm of Confidence

The vigorous psalm which follows was expressed at a time when Nephi was needing to feel confident. Lehi, after completing his farewell counsel and his benedictions on his sons, had died. Nephi's older brothers were bent on turning against him, and he was also aware of his own shortcomings (II Nephi 3:31-33). Then he remembered the gracious love of God and thought of the help available. He asked himself, "Why should my heart weep . . . and my strength slacken because of my afflictions?" He sang this hymn which might be called, "Rejoice, O My Heart!" (II Nephi 3:50). This is a summarized restating of the longer hymn beginning with II Nephi 3:31.

My soul delighteth in the things of the Lord;
and my heart pondereth upon the things
which I have seen and heard.
Nevertheless, notwithstanding the great goodness
of the Lord
in showing me his great and marvelous works,
my heart exclaimeth, "O wretched man that I am!"
My soul grieveth because of mine iniquities.

Yet I know in whom I have trusted:
My God hath been my support.
He hath led me through
    mine afflictions in the wilderness,
and he hath preserved me
    upon the waters of the great deep.
He has filled me with his love.

If, then, I have seen so great things,
if the Lord hath visited me in so much mercy,
why should my soul linger in the valley of sorrow?

Awake, my soul! No longer droop in sin!
Rejoice, O my heart, and give no more place
    for the enemy of my soul.
Do not slacken my strength
    because of my afflictions.

Rejoice, O my heart,
yea, rejoice in my God,
in the Rock of my salvation.

Ammon's Testimonial Review of Mission Ministry

Nothing in scripture surpasses Ammon's expression of joy
and satisfaction in missionary ministry. The sons of King
Mosiah had relinquished their princeships and had gone on a
rigorous mission to the Lamanites as related in previous
chapters. Now after fourteen years they are reviewing what
had taken place. Ammon bursts forth in exuberant joy.

In brotherly remonstrance Aaron said, "Ammon, I fear
that your joy is carrying you away to boasting" (Alma
14:90). Ammon replied, "I do not boast in my own strength,

in my own wisdom. My heart is full of joy to the brim. I am rejoicing in God. I will boast of my God, for in his strength I can do all things. . . . If this is boasting, I will boast."

This is a summary selection from the longer testimonial review. The original is found in Alma 14:79 ff.

My brothers, how great reason have we to rejoice!
Could we have supposed
when we started from the land of Zarahemla
that God would have granted us such blessings?

Our brothers the Lamanites were in darkness!
Now how many of them are brought
to behold the marvelous light of God!

If we had not come up
out of the land of Zarahemla,
these brothers who now love us
would still be racked with hatred against us;
yea, they would also be strangers to God.

How many thousands of our brothers
are loosed from the pains of hell,
and are brought to sing redeeming love,
because of the power of God's word which is in us!

Do you remember, my brothers,
when we said we were going
to the land of Nephi,
to preach unto our brothers the Lamanites,
how those in Zarahemla laughed us to scorn?
They even said, Let us take up arms against them!

We went into the wilderness,
not to destroy our brothers
but with intent to save some few of their souls.

We have entered into their homes and taught them.
We have taught them in their streets,
upon their hills,
in their temples, and in their synagogues.

We have been cast out, mocked, and smitten;
we have been stoned, bound with cords,
and cast in prison.
Through the power and wisdom of God
we have been delivered.

Now many of them have buried
their weapons of war, in the earth,
because of their love for their brothers.

This is the blessing
which has been bestowed upon us,
that we have been instruments in the hands of God
to bring about this great work.

Now, my brothers, we see
that God is mindful of every people,
in whatever land they may be in.

This is my life and my light,
my joy and my salvation.
I will give thanks to God forever. Amen.

The Warning of Samuel the Lamanite

The fifth chapter of the Book of Helaman opens with a description of the comparative conditions of Lamanites and Nephites. The Nephites were reveling in their material prosperity. They were confident of their ability to manage things their own way. They were not concerned about what God wanted them to be doing. It was appropriate that a prophet should cry out in warning, "Woe unto this great city of Zarahemla!" On the whole the Zarahemlites were in no mood to listen. In their thinking they were getting along all right. Such a warning prophet would be considered a disturbing nuisance. Samuel reminds us of the biblical Elijah in ancient Israel; he would dart in, deliver his message, and then leave.

Samuel, a Lamanite, came into the land of Zarahemla, and began to preach. He preached repentance, for the Nephites were in great wickedness. The people cast him out. He was about to return to his own land, but the voice of the Lord came unto him, that he should return again.

The people would not suffer him to enter the city, so he got upon the wall, stretched forth his hand, and cried with a loud voice. He prophesied what the Lord put into his heart: "I was sent unto you, that you might have glad tidings, but you would not receive me. Because of the hardness of the hearts of the people of Nephi, heavy destruction awaits this people, except you repent.

"Your riches are cursed because you have set your heart on them, and have not hearkened unto the words of him who gave them to you. Your days of probation are past; you have procrastinated the day of your salvation; now your destruction is made sure. After five years the Son of God will come to earth, to redeem all those who believe on his name. I give you a sign of his coming: There shall be great lights in the heavens, and a new star shall arise.

"God has commanded me to come to you, and tell you this, and say, 'Cry unto this people, Repent and prepare the way of the Lord.'"

Nephi had been going among the people, preaching, crying repentance, baptizing, that they might know that the Christ must come shortly. As many as believed the words of Samuel went forth unto him, to be baptized, but the greater part of the people did not believe Samuel. They threw stones at him.

When they were not able to hit Samuel with their stones and arrows, they cried out to their captains, "Take this fellow and bind him, for he is a devil! Because of the power of the devil in him, we cannot hit him." They went forth to lay their hands on him, but he cast himself down from the wall, and fled out of their lands.

He went to his own country, and began to preach and prophesy among his own people. Samuel was never heard of again among the Nephites.

The Golden Age of the Nephites

The foremost happening narrated in the Book of Mormon is the visitation of Jesus Christ and his ministry among the peoples on the Western continent. In our explorations two classic readings from this story have been included, the story of the arrival and the message about the "other sheep." Other readings may be found in III Nephi, chapters five and following. These passages sound much like the teachings and ministries of Jesus in Judea and Galilee, as would be expected. There is this difference: In the Land Bountiful ministry was confined to a somewhat restricted group.

After the departure of Jesus there was a period of enthusiastic evangelizing. There was another story taking place—the developing of a Zionic community, the emergence of a society of Christian brotherhood. It would be sounder to say that these developments were two facets of a single development. Zionic living and evangelistic expression are not separable. Explorers in the class should take time to celebrate this Zionic happening. The beautiful, though abbreviated, story is found in IV Nephi. Many wish that the life of these two hundred years was more adequately described.

There is a sequel to this golden age that is worthy of consideration. What happened that undermined the Zionic society? Did Christians come to take their community for granted? Did goodness become passive while evil became aggressive? Did their orderly way of living and their industry produce a society in which financial values became paramount? Did the goodness of the society lack appeal for persons of action? Was the way of life too peaceful? In time the story says, "There was a great division among the people" (IV Nephi 1:39). Here is a challenging reminder that Zion is a matter of continuing as well as of originating.

The Bible picture which is the nearest replica of the Book of Mormon Zionic era appears in the closing part of the second chapter of Acts, the picture of the Jerusalem community of Christians after the Day of Pentecost. Here, too, was a combining of Zionic community living and evangelistic outreach. "The Lord added to the church daily." This must also have taken place in the Land Bountiful after their time of Pentecost when Jesus Christ was with them. This following material is adapted from IV Nephi.

> Those who believed went forth
> unto all the people of Nephi,
> and preached the gospel of Christ
> unto all the people on the face of the
>   land.

And the people were converted unto the Lord,
and were united unto the Church of Christ.

By the thirty-sixth year the people
were all converted unto the Lord,
both Nephites and Lamanites.

There were no contentions and disputations
        among them,
        and every man did deal justly
        with one another.

They had all things in common among them;
there were no rich and no poor,
no bond and free—all were free.

The Lord prospered them exceedingly in the land;
they built up cities where cities had burned.
Even did they build again the great city Zarahemla.

The people of Nephi waxed strong, and increased,
and became a fair and a delightsome people.

They married and were given in marriage,
and were blessed according to the promises
that God had made to them.

They walked after the commandments
which they had received from God,
meeting often together, both to pray and to hear
the word of the Lord.

There were no contentions in the land,
because of the love of God which dwelt
in the hearts of the people.

There were no robbers, no murderers,
neither were there Lamanites, nor any manner of ites;
they were one, the children of God.

And surely there could not be a happier people,
among all the people
who had been created by the hand of God.

Considerations for Conversation

In this exploration we have lived with passages that speak graphically and effectively of problems and situations that concerned those of former years. We want to discover what these can say to us for living in our day.

1. What did Alma say about the dynamic nature of faith? With what notions about faith does his description stand in contrast? How do the words "experiment" and "exercise" speak functionally today? What are some key phrases in his treatise? How did his Rameumptom experience with the Zoramites stimulate him to make this interpretation of faith? After conversation about Alma's message, let the class read aloud, together, the passage arranged for the text. Let it be considered an affirmation of faith.

2. What had been the motivations of Ammon and his three brothers in going on their missionary project among the Lamanites? What qualities were required in them? What methods did they employ? What was the foundation for Ammon's gladness and satisfaction? Where and how might such an Ammon carry on such a missionary venture in our

church today? What other names of past and present would you put on the roster of adventuring missionaries with Ammon's name? After getting acquainted with Ammon, read the selected passage together.

3. What kind of faith, what kind of love, what kind of diligence characterized the "golden age of the Nephites"? What do you think brought about the decline of their Zionic community? How do you envision the living together of Nephites and Lamanites? How did the emergence of "ites" enter into the deterioration of the community? After pointing up the constructive forces and the spiritual fraternity and the sense of evangelistic mission of the community, read aloud together this abridged picture of "the golden age" of the Nephites.

4. Following are selected quotations from the Book of Mormon. What was the setting out of which they emerged? What was the original speaker aiming to say? What do they suggest to us today about living in our modern times?

a. "Do not let us be slothful because of the easiness of the way."—Alma 17:81.

b. "By small means, the Lord can bring about great things."—I Nephi 5:36.

c. "Their sorrowing . . . was the sorrowing of the damned, because the Lord would not always suffer them to take happiness in sin."—Mormon 1:37.

d. "Wickedness never was happiness."—Alma 19:74.

e. "Make it your law to do business by the voice of the people."—Mosiah 13:36.

f. "And the Lord said, 'Go to work and build.' "—Ether 1:43.

g. "To be learned is good, if they hearken unto the counsels of God."—II Nephi 6:61.

5. When Jesus Christ first appeared in Land Bountiful, he said, "I am the light and the life of the world" (III Nephi 5:12). He said to these people what he had said in Judah and Galilee: "Let your light so shine before this people..." (III Nephi 5:63). What does this quotation contribute to this teaching about spiritual light: "I am the light which you shall hold up, that which you have seen me do" (III Nephi 8:55). How does this make light an active, creative force? How does this focus on the doing Christ? This conception of Jesus Christ expresses what he is in the Book of Mormon—more than a name, more than an abstraction, more than a symbol, more than a historical figure.

6. If you were to work out a selection of choice passages from the Book of Mormon for a brochure for interested persons to read so they would catch the merit and the message of the book, what passages would you select and on what basis would you select them? What introductory statements would you make? What passages or quotations would you choose for a sound and artistic portrayal of the nature and workings of God? What passages would you select that picture saintly living?

7. What passages would you include in your collection that speak of living the good life here and now on this earth, utilizing the resources that God places at our disposal? One man commented that an appeal of the Book of Mormon to him was its call to live here and now, not a "wait-until-you-get-to-heaven" preaching. Where do you find this in the book?

8. What passages would you choose that would throw light on Nephi's comment, "And it came to pass that we lived after the manner of happiness" (II Nephi 4:43). What other quotations refer to "the manner of happiness"?

9. What qualities constitute spiritual artistry in a passage of scripture? What do these comments say: "It sounds good but it is gushy," and "What he is getting at is good, but couldn't he get at it better?"

10. One loyal believer in the Book of Mormon observes, "The ranking quotation in the Book of Mormon, for me, is in the foreword, 'Jesus is the Christ, the Eternal God, manifesting himself to all nations.'" In what way and to what extent do you accord with his choice?

Exploration XI. The Book Bridges Color Cleavage . . . The book speaks of tensions with color and culture involved. This is done in pre-modern conceptions. There is need to explore carefully, lest there be unsound presumptions.

Yes, in the Book of Mormon there are severe problems in the field of skin coloration. Sometimes this comes to the fore as a major theme of the story. Between those with a dark skin and those with a "fair" skin hostility was often intense and active. Careful reading of the story indicates that several factors were involved in this hostility. Conflicts showed tensions over differences in culture, differences in religion, differences over possession of lands. This reminds us of the complexity of factors in racial conflicts in modern times.

The Nephites and Lamanites retained stories from the past. These helped to keep alive feelings of social distance and to rationalize positions of both sides. Long ago, said their traditions, there was a split that involved injustice and robbery. The wrongs were never righted, so the conflicts had to continue. It was something like the rift between the Israelites and the Edomites. The hostility between Jacob and Esau lived on. Jews and Arabs kept alive the rift that took place when Hagar and her son Ishmael were ousted by Sarah, wife of Abraham. The Book of Mormon depicts this kind of thing happening. To be a Lamanite or to be a Nephite was sufficient ground for suspicion, sometimes for death.

There were times when the two peoples were brought together in partial or inclusive friendly relationships, or in complete suspension of ill feeling. Sometimes a segment of the Lamanites would join with the Nephites. The book is honest in portraying the troubles caused by this color tension. It pictures, too, how the story closes with tragedy that grew out of this and related tensions. There is no Pollyanna solution, but there is affirmation that solution is possible, that harmony can be achieved. The Book of Mormon is unique in picturing how two peoples did at times surmount their hostilities and did live together in peace, sometimes as one people. When they did so, the uniting factor was spiritual.

Presumptions from the Bible

There are many differences between what the Bible says and what persons say the Bible says. When a notion gets grounded that such-and-such a thing is said in the Bible, this notion is often passed on with considerable insistency. And if this notion substantiates some idea the believers want to support, they may grab hold of a doctrine or datum or parable and play it to the full. This has happened in matters of race and race relationships.

The traditions about Ham have been many. Generally readers have gone back to the story of Noah and his three sons, some time after the flood. This was remembered as taking place when Noah imbibed too freely of some strong wine, became intoxicated, and lay in his tent without benefit of clothing. Ham was designated as cursed for his lack of respect for his father. The book of Genesis contained the strong line, "Cursed be Canaan [son of Ham]; a servant of servants shall he be unto his brethren" (Genesis 9:29). So Ham and his descendants came to be considered doubly cursed—with blackness and with servitude. In many places, with many people, this was taken as pure gospel. What is more, many considered it their duty to help carry out the cursing.

In general, such a view carried a basic postulate—the desirability and priority of whiteness. Generally God was pictured as altogether white with such features of nose and lips as a "good white man" might have. His hair was presumed to be straight or wavy. Angels were pictured as white in color, and wearing white robes. Today in some countries where the missionaries who brought Christianity to a locale were white, those who play the role of angels in dramas and tableaux are daubed with makeup to show angelic whiteness. Sometimes the notion has been expressed that the skin of persons who truly live as Christians might someday be changed to white.

It is not unlikely that persons who have these notions about the Bible will bring these notions with them as they read the Book of Mormon. That whiteness rates higher than darkness is assumed to be God's way. Generally this darkness has been thought of as punishment for some misconduct with color and consequences transmitted to succeeding generations. The sons of Ham and the sons of Laman are seen as being in similar predicament.

The Book of Mormon has not been free from this kind of interpretation. However, when it is allowed to speak in fullness, this book speaks otherwise. It points the way to a community of living that transcends all this division and conflict.

A Case with a Problem

A young couple of Negro blood were baptized into the

Reorganized Church of Jesus Christ of Latter Day Saints. They were thrilled with the gospel of love and evangelistic mission to all the world, to all peoples. Then a block came. They confessed that they could not see their way clear to bring any of their friends with dark skin into any of our church meetings. Especially were they reluctant to bring their friends if the Book of Mormon was going to be considered. This book was the source of their difficulty. They had gone to some classes where the book was being used for study. From the first, the class got involved in the Laman-Nephi conflict. They started with the first book of Nephi. The sins of Laman and his followers and the placing of the curse of a dark skin were duly noted. The darkness of skin of the disobedient Lamanites was interpreted as representing the darkness of their souls. The two Negroes came to feel that they could not hold out this book to their friends with black skin. And they still had to face the problem concerning themselves. What was their standing with God? Were they second-rate Saints? Had their forebears been disobedient and received a curse?

Two fields were explored. One involved a clear looking into the Book of Mormon. The couple came to see that many things had been read into the book in matters of race and skin color. The records of long ago had been concerned with identification of the people who had strayed. If the prevailing color had been black the identifying mark might have been whiteness. The difference, not the specific color, was what had interested the first narrators. They saw how words such as "fair" had become associated with lightness. They sensed how those who had taught the class had said too much; they had said more than the book said.

The other field involved an experience in the kind of fellowship that transcends racial barriers. These two met a patriarch and a pastor in a church sanctuary for their patriarchal blessings, and God was with them. It was a Pentecost Day experience. As on that first day in Jerusalem (Acts 2) all fences of race and color went down. Two blacks and two whites met in spiritual fellowship, bonded by the Spirit of God. There was "one accord." Here the two of darker skin met the Universal Christ of the Book of Mormon.

The Nephites' Conception of Their Calling

The Nephite recorders had a keen sense of purpose in their migration from Jerusalem to the Western land. They were to carry out a mission for God. They saw the Lamanites dropping out and turning against this purpose. They wrote about (1) the spiritual decline of the Lamanites; (2) the war-inclined genius of the Lamanites; (3) the necessity to avoid mixing with the Lamanites in their Lamanite ways; and (4) the darkened condition of the Lamanites. This prompted the Nephites to stay away from the Lamanites for their own physical security, their cultural identity, and their spiritual integrity.

This gave the Nephite prophets a sense of assignment for keeping their own people in good spiritual condition. They were to fulfill their calling in coming to the "land of promise." They were to function in God's longtime program of using the Jews as "chosen people" to express God to all the world. These prophets advised their fellow Nephites that should they fail in their calling, they would go down in disaster and forfeit their right to receive help from God.

Bans on Intermarriage

The early part of the Old Testament has many passages that direct the Hebrews against marrying those who were other than Hebrews. Marriage with the Canaanites was expressly forbidden. This was the general rule of most tribes in matters of extra-group marriage. The blood would be weakened. The faith would be exposed to heathenism. The property could be dissipated. The family name and strain would be less than pure. The migrants from Jerusalem brought these outlooks with them. They faced enough difficulty in maintaining good faith in God without adding to the strain by mating with nonbelievers.

Early Christians had directives in this matter. Paul wrote to the congregation in Corinth, "Do not be mismated with unbelievers. For what partnership have righteousness and unrighteousness? Or what fellowship has light and darkness? Or what has a believer in common with an unbeliever?" (II Corinthians 6:14, 15). It was pretty clear to Paul that a Christian should not marry a pagan. Such a marriage might lead to the Christian husband or wife's becoming detached from the Christian faith and fellowship. The social relationships of those who were Christians and those who were non-Christian were different. The Christian's life is centered in Christ. This would not be meaningful to a pagan. This outlook would apply to the Nephites as they looked at the way of living of the Lamanites.

Concern in this matter is expressed in our church's document on marriage (Doctrine and Covenants 111). The church formulated the statement that there was to be no prohibiting of members "marrying out of the church"— choice is with the person. But there follows a warning against such extra-church marriage. There is a presumed strain when a husband or wife cannot or does not share with his or her companion the faith that is the core in living. The ancients were aware of this problem.

The Nephites looked upon marriage with Lamanites as dangerous to faith, as destructive in tone of living.

Nephite Writers Spoke Their Warnings

The early Nephite recorders placed the responsibility on the Lamanites themselves. The Lamanites withdrew from the Lord; it was not the Lord who withdrew from them. They brought disasters on themselves. This statement was made shortly after the withdrawal of the Nephites from the Lamanites:

"They had hardened their hearts against the Lord, so that they had become like flint. They had been white, and exceedingly fair and delightsome; but now, that they might not be enticing unto my people, the Lord God caused a skin of blackness to come upon them. And cursed shall be the seed of him who mixes with their seed; they shall be cursed with the same cursing. . . .

"Because of their cursing which was upon them, they became an idle people, full of mischief and subtlety; and they sought in the wilderness for beasts of prey."—Adapted from II Nephi 4:34 ff.

In fairness, let it be remembered that when Jacob was talking to his people about the kind of family living they should be developing, he pointed out that "the Lamanites, your brothers whom you hate" were doing better in their family living than were the Nephites. These Lamanites had a one-husband-with-one-wife arrangement and the parents loved their children.

Enos, the son of Jacob, gave a picture of the Lamanites as a live-in-the-woods people. In his day the breach between the two peoples was wide and deep.

"I bear record that the people of Nephi did seek diligently to restore the Lamanites unto the true faith in God. But our labors were vain; their hatred was fixed, and they were led by their evil nature, that they became wild, and ferocious, and a bloodthirsty people; full of idolatry, and filthiness.

"They fed upon beasts of prey; they dwelt in tents, and wandered about in the wilderness, with a short skin girted about their loins, with their heads shaven. Their skill was in the bow, and the cimeter, and the ax. Many of them ate nothing but raw meat; and they were continually seeking to destroy us."—Adapted from Enos 1:30 ff.

By this time conditions resembled a feud between two gangs or families in mountaineer country. No charge had to be made except that a man was a member of the other group. The name alone was enough to brand the accused person. A person of the out-group threatens the security of the in-group. In Appalachian lore, all the evidence the Hatfields needed to convict a man was that he was a McCoy. In ancient America a Nephite was seized and bound because he was a Nephite (Alma 12:30).

The writers of the Nephite story spoke of "the curse" as self-incurred. They also considered the curse as cumulative and increasing. Their persistence in a way of life widened the breach between the two peoples and necessitated caution in inter-association. This was Alma's affirmation: "Now I would that you see that they brought upon themselves the curse; even so does every man that is cursed bring upon himself his own condemnation" (Alma 1:119, 120).

The Beginnings of the American Indian

Many notions have grown up about the ethnology of the American Indian. Some of these beliefs and traditions have been woven into the story of the Book of Mormon by members of our church. Some say the Book of Mormon declares that the American Indians have all come from the people who migrated from Jerusalem. The book does not say this. Readers put together this or that theory. After awhile these theories are assumed to be clearly stated in the book.

The Book of Mormon speaks of a people, the Lamanites, who annihilated the Nephite forces in the fourth century after Christ. There the story closed. The book of happenings is reopened when Christopher Columbus sailed across the Atlantic Ocean and landed in October 1492 on one of the islands we now call the West Indies. He had been searching for a route to the East Indies and thought that he had found it. So he called the people Indians.

Theories evolved about these darkskinned people of the new land. Then, as now, many persons wanted a simple, inclusive explanation. The Spaniards in particular rated these aborigines pretty low. The European conquerors believed that the religion and culture of the Indians should be replaced by the faith and ways of the white man. The two groups seldom were able to live together in peace.

Believers in the Book of Mormon identified the American Indians as having Lamanite origin, making them Hebrew in stock. Others speculated that they might be of "the lost tribes of Israel." Often an inclusive application was made: all peoples of the Western Hemisphere came of Lamanite beginnings. The Book of Mormon did not and could not make such an affirmation. It is one thing to say that Lamanite blood and culture went into the American Indian; it is something else to assign monopoly to this. Today many inquiring believers in the Book of Mormon leave place for migrations across the Bering Straits area with consequent inclusion of Oriental blood and culture in peoples of North America. Here again it is only fair to let the book speak for itself without reading into it what it does not say.

Times of Evangelistic Unity

The Book of Mormon brings to the fore the possibility

and hope of resolving strains and conflicts between two peoples. So intense was the hostility between the Lamanites and the Nephites that fear and hatred became automatic. When Ammon entered the land of Ishmael the Lamanites "took him and bound him, as was their custom, to bind all the Nephites who fell into their hands." Awareness of this hostility heightens appreciation of the times when this was overcome, when evangelistic contacts turned out well. This is best exemplified by the missionary ministry of the sons of Mosiah among the Lamanites. The Lamanites who were converted changed their way of living and chose a name other than Lamanite (Alma 14:19). "They began to be a very industrious people; yea, and they were friendly with the Nephites; therefore they opened a correspondence with them, and the curse of God no more followed them" (Alma 14:20).

So thorough was the conversion of the Lamanites that they renounced warring. "Now there was not one soul among all the people who had been converted unto the Lord, that would take up arms against their brethren; they would not even make any preparations for war" (Alma 14:27). Later when Ammon reviewed what had taken place in their mission among the Lamanites, he said, "Behold, how many of them are brought to behold the marvelous light of God!" (Alma 14:81).

These converted Lamanites, ever in danger at the hands of their countrymen, migrated to the land of Jershon (Alma 15:23). The Nephite recorder said of them,

"They were called by the Nephites the people of Ammon; . . . they were among the people of Nephi, and also numbered among the people who were of the church of God. And they were also distinguished for their zeal towards God, and also towards men; for they were perfectly honest and upright in all things; and they were firm in the faith of Christ. . . . They never could be prevailed upon to take up arms against their brethren."—Alma 15:29-32.

A Lamanite Prophesies to Nephites

Once when the Nephites "did still remain in wickedness" there came to the land of Zarahemla the prophet Samuel, a Lamanite (see Helaman 5). Some were moved by his preaching and were baptized by the Nephite minister Nephi (Helaman 5:116). This happening indicates that not all the iniquity was on one side with righteousness on the other. People were evaluated according to what they were as persons, not by their membership in the Lamanite or the Nephite nation. The Book of Mormon is strong in stressing that a man stands on his merits and is to be judged according to his own character.

The Golden Age of Ancient America

Jesus Christ charged his disciples with a universal commission. He came to the Nephites that he might minister to those more ready for his coming. He instructed them, "Go ye into all the world, and preach the gospel to every creature" (Mormon 4:86). There were to be no barriers, no restrictions. The result was that "The people were all converted unto the Lord, upon all the face of the land, both Nephites and Lamanites, and there were no contentions and disputations among them" (IV Nephi 1:3). This was the simple, frank description, "There were no Lamanites, nor any manner of ites, but they were one, the children of Christ" (IV Nephi 1:20). In this account is the glorious sentence, "And surely there could not be a happier people among all the people who had been created by the hand of God" (verse 19).

For about two hundred years the people were united

without designating some Nephites and some Lamanites. This "golden age" is the Book of Mormon picture of what can take place as nations get together with God. The record says that such an age was possible "because of the love of God which did dwell in the hearts of the people" (verse 17). This love was centered in Christ and stimulated by Christ to practical expression.

Again Contending Nations

Decline began to take place as social dissension arose. This started in a spiritual breaking away. "A small part of the people . . . revolted from the church, and took upon them the name of Lamanites" (verse 23). Pride and pretense came to the fore. What we might call a humanistic church appeared, a church which "denied the Christ" (verse 31). This group turned against those who did believe in Christ. Religion became divisive; the former unity was gone. By A.D. 300 the rift was complete.

And Then Only the Lamanites

The story of the spiritual decline of the Nephites, their fighting with the Lamanites, and their destruction is told in the sub-book which also carries the name "The Book of Mormon." Mormon, as a young man, became the military leader of the Nephites. He said of the Nephites, "They hardened their hearts against the Lord their God" (Mormon 1:67). When the Nephites lost, they mourned in complaint; when they won, they began to "boast in their own strength" (verse 74). Both Nephites and Lamanites "delighted in the shedding of blood" (Mormon 2:13).

The final battle took place at Hill Cumorah (Mormon 3:3). The Lamanites mowed down the Nephites; only a handful were left. In time Moroni, son of Mormon, became the lone survivor. The story of the Nephites was closed. The Lamanites were possessors of the land, and they kept no written records.

Moderns in the Western Hemisphere are wondering what to do about the people we call American Indians. The Book of Mormon affirms that Gentiles of the Church of Jesus Christ have a mission to these natives, a mission of friendship in Christ.

Some Basic Guidelines in the Book of Mormon

1. Groups can transcend their differences in appearance and culture as they are united in common loyalty in Jesus Christ. Such a harmonizing loyalty is required. Nephites and Lamanites lived together in Christian fraternity as long as they nurtured this functioning loyalty.

2. Difference in color and related matters are not to be so emphasized that they become dividing factors. Biological appearance is secondary to spiritual genuineness. Jacob warned his own people against conceit in their appearance. He gave this straightforward directive to his people, "A commandment I give unto you, which is the word of God, that you revile no more against them, because of the darkness of their skins" (Jacob 2:60). He advised his people to be concerned about their own spiritual filthiness rather than with the biological dirtiness of the Lamanites.

3. Differentiations between peoples should be made in relation to qualities of character, to ways of living, to vitality of faith rather than to external appearance. The avoidance of Lamanites was to protect and strengthen the Nephite mission. In time the Nephites should be strong enough to reach out to and consociate with the Lamanites.

4. God uses and commissions peoples for stewardships in his ongoing program. He endows them in accordance with the

requirements for their assignment and their application to their assignments. A people is chosen for a mission. If the people fail in their stewardship, they lose right to subsidy and support.

5. The consequences of evildoing continue from generation to generation. The blame, the guilt, is not transmitted. God calls his people to build communities with wholesome influence and creativity that contribute to clean living. God looks to the development of social living of Zionic quality.

6. God covenants with a people for the use of a land and its resources for righteous living. Such a country is a "land of promise." If iniquity "abounds" the people forfeit the promise of God to sustain them. "Unto the righteous it shall be blessed forever" (II Nephi 1:15).

7. People in spiritual and cultural decline are remembered and will be ministered to as they are ready and as the time is ripe. In the Book of Mormon this applies particularly to the surviving Lamanites.

8. Continuing vigilance and expanding vision are required to maintain Zionic community. There is no once-and-for-always establishment and continuance. The Nephites achieved a condition that was happy and healthy in the days of Captain Moroni (Alma 22:24), but this declined with loss of sense of national mission and with weakening of working communion with God. This happened, too, after the golden age of the Nephites. Zion can never be taken for granted. Alma warned Helaman, "Do not let us be slothful because of the easiness of the way" (Alma 17:81).

9. A people breaks down through internal decline with loss of spiritual values, spiritual vision, spiritual vitality. These precede apparent collapse before external forces. The Nephites were not worthy or able to endure before the onslaught of the Lamanites in the closing struggle. Arnold

Toynbee once said, "The chief danger to man is man." He commented that most civilizations in the past have broken down "through their own acts" before any outside or "alien force" dealt them a "mortal blow."

10. People have to have a cause, a mission, to live for that is greater than themselves. Dr. Toynbee refers to the fact that a civilization must have its creative minorities who work for the good of the whole. When the minority gets concerned with its own self, with its own security, with its own institutionalism, its spiritual function ends. When either Nephites or Lamanites became primarily concerned with their own self-centered affairs they lost reason for living and got into conflict with others. A civilization needs continual spiritual transformation. When a people live well spiritually, their industry and consistency will bring good living conditions in spiritual matters. The Book of Mormon says many times that when the people, whether Lamanite or Nephite, live godly lives, they do well in material matters. Mormon once spoke of "prosperity in Christ" (IV Nephi 1:26).

11. The motivation for people-with-people association is brotherliness for the common good, not aggressive mastery or exploitation of materials. The Nephites are described as having "great joy because of the conversion of the Lamanites." The satisfaction was in their new, deepening fellowship together with Christ. This was the comment: "They did fellowship one with another, and did rejoice with one another" (Helaman 2:120, 121).

12. All peoples are included in God's ongoing program, with intent to achieve a world brotherhood of God's sons and daughters. This is stated early in the Book of Mormon and this was the intent of the book: "to the convincing of the Jew and the Gentile that Jesus is the Christ, the Eternal God, manifesting himself unto all nations."

Considerations for Conversation

1. What social factors made it advisable for a strong stand to be taken against marriage between Jews and non-Jews when the Hebrews migrated into Canaan? How would intermarriage have endangered the Hebrew faith and threatened their mission to the world? Was this a basic consideration on the part of the Nephites in their relationships with the Lamanites?

2. What connotation do you make for the word "fair" in the Book of Mormon? What does it mean in this reference to "the people of Nephi" in the "golden age" when they were described as becoming "an exceeding fair and delightsome people" (IV Nephi 1:11)? What does "fair" mean as used here?

3. There are some believers in the Book of Mormon who explain the color problem as having its origin in the "preexistent" world. These say that some "spirits" were "disobedient" and had to be punished and cast aside, so they were born on the earth with a darker skin. It is further added that the curse would deprive them of priesthood and "full celestial glory." What are presumptions about whiteness and dark color in such a theory? What conceptions of God are associated?

4. How did Ammon and his brothers develop rapport with the Lamanites? Is there any mention of "the color problem"? What emphases and experiences brought the Lamanites and the Nephites together in common fraternity? What pointers might this give us for our race-with-race relationships today? What time element was involved?

5. What is your reaction to this happening: An American Indian who became a member of the Restoration Church was told by an elder who believed that God favors whiteness that if he would be faithful, his skin would become "fair and

light." The American Indian replied, "I have no desire to become a paleface."

6. What is your response to the comment of a dark-skinned person concerning the dream of there being "one fold and one shepherd," "Will there be different pens for sheep of different color?"

7. How would you interpret the Book of Mormon to a person of dark skin who sees it as denouncing darkness of skin and elevating whiteness of skin?

8. What do you identify as the theology of Latter Day Saints in the field of ethnology? (Consult Conversation Nineteen in *When Teen-agers Talk Theology* by R. A. Cheville. Note the "affirmation in ethnology," page 341.) How does the Book of Mormon help or hinder in this field?

9. What bearing does the story of Samuel the Lamanite have upon your conception of the relationship of race and religion, of color and commission?

10. What relationship to the problem of color may the rising up of self-interest groups have on the whole situation? The record says that in "the golden age" there were no "Lamanites, nor any manner of ites" (IV Nephi 1:20). How may a color or culture or other group contribute to the total welfare and when may these "ites" get in the way and promote division and hostility? How can we have harmony with diversity?

11. What values does the Book of Mormon at its best put forth which would stimulate and bring to pass the achieving of a social order that transcends social animosities that divide? What are these spiritual values?

Exploration XII. The Book Continues

Chapters in a Continuing Story . . . The past is prelude. The story of the peoples in the book is expected to continue. All this applies to the present.

Any book written about what God is doing will round out with this statement, "To be continued." Where God is concerned, there is no last chapter followed by the word "Finis." God is not going to be emeritus with a "has been" outlook on what he has been doing to date.

Some books of scripture do have a rounding-out mood and outlook. Some have a scheduled eschatology, with a fairly specific listing of events to happen. Some look to "the end of time" when all problems will be solved and all distress removed. There will be an unchanging heaven for persons who have lined up with God and lived his way. However, there are differences in thinking as to what constitutes this right way. Often heaven's goodness is thought of as coming automatically, with God providing for all needs, eternally. This outlook brings on differing reactions. Some get to work to hasten the day of the coming of the end. Others are of the mind that no man knows the day nor the hour and that all man can do is wait.

What of the Book of Mormon?

This book is not of the wait-for-heaven type. Nor is it a speculate-about-paradise production. In this book there is no place for those who say, "Let God do it!" The gospel of this book is that of working with God in his ongoing endeavor. The children of God are to find satisfaction in their working, as God does. There is no creed for the lazy man in the Book of Mormon.

In closing, Moroni wrote an admonition to his fellow Jews, bidding them to get to work with God and bring to pass what God has in mind for them and for all. This was his call to his people, a call to be getting on with God:

"Awake, and arise from the dust, O Jerusalem! . . . Strengthen your stakes, and enlarge your borders forever, that you may no more be confounded, that the covenants of the eternal Father which he has made to you, O house of Israel, may be fulfilled."—Moroni 10:28.

Moroni and his father Mormon had seen their people wiped out by the slaughtering Lamanites. The battle of Cumorah had brought to a close the story of the Nephites. But neither man thought of God as bringing the curtain down on what was to happen on the Western continent and in the world. Neither thought of God surrendering to the forces that had brought setback in his plans for the given time. For them the works of God would not be frustrated. The story would continue.

Here again we open the book to let it speak for itself, in its own way. This voice will be spoken before the days of the Gregorian calendar, before the advancing of the view that the earth is round and the universe is more than earth-centered. All this speaks before much is known about the movements of the planets, about space-in-universe. We shall see how this book looks at things to come. This much is clear: the story continues.

1. *The Western land would be kept from the knowledge of men until the time when it would be expedient in God's plan for its discovery and settlement.*

The Book of Mormon carries the theology that Paul expressed in his message on Mars' Hill: God appoints the time and circumstances for the locating and landing on lands of God's earth. In this vein Nephi wrote: "It is wisdom that this land should be kept as yet from the knowledge of other nations; for many nations would overrun the land, that there would be no place for an inheritance" (II Nephi 1:16, 17). The timing of the discovery would fit into God's longtime program.

Nephi said, too, that those who would be brought to this Western land would be those Gentiles who would come for purposes of freedom. It would be as if they were coming "out of captivity" (I Nephi 3:155). The story of the settlement of North America tells of those who came for political freedom, economic freedom, intellectual freedom, religious freedom. America did not open up until these movements for freedom were getting a good start in Europe. The firstcomers were those who were wanting to get away from oppressing conditions. Many of them had conviction that something good was going to happen in the new land. Significantly, in faith, John Robinson could tell his fellows in Leyden, "The Lord has more light and truth yet to break forth."

Nephi wrote another pointed prediction. God would move upon a man of exploring spirit and direct him to the Western Hemisphere. The story of the conceptions and convictions of Christopher Columbus reads like the biography of a God-inspired prophet. Joaquin Miller caught something of this driving will when he wrote that Columbus kept saying, "Sail on!" This is the portrayal by Nephi of this man's mission and ways:

> "I looked and beheld a man among the Gentiles, who was separated from the seed of my brethren by the many waters; and I beheld the Spirit of God, that it came down and wrought upon the man; and he went forth upon the many waters, even to the seed of my brethren, who were in the promised land."—I Nephi 3:147.

The main thing here is not to identify all the details of Columbus' voyage; rather the thing to note is that these men of ancient times were looking forward in hope. The land would be discovered and opened for settlement in God's own good time. The discovery and exploration would be by Gentiles.

2. *The Jews as chosen people would accept their mission in due time, coming to know the Christ, his gospel, his church through the ministry of Gentiles.*

The fate of the Jews always concerned the prophets of the Western lands. God had brought them to "the land of promise" for purposes, but the poor conduct of the once chosen people had removed them from their calling. Was all hope gone? By the time the book closed the Nephites had been exterminated and the Lamanites were wild and decadent. Was everything of promise lost for the Jews?

The analogy of the olive tree is prominent in the book. It is the symbol used to indicate how things would be coming out. This analogy is explained in I Nephi 3:16 ff. The Gentiles and "the house of Israel" are compared "to an olive tree whose branches should be broken off and should be scattered upon all the face of the earth." One of these branches had been led to "the land of promise" (verse 17). The Gentiles were interpreted as a branch "grafted in." Later Nephi wrote how the gospel would come to the Gentiles and then through them to "the remnant" of Nephi's people. The grafted branches would bring the message of the Messiah to the natural branches.

"In the latter days, when our seed shall have dwindled in unbelief, even for the space of many years and many generations after the Messiah shall be manifested in body to the children of men, then shall the fullness of the gospel of the Messiah come to the Gentiles, and from the Gentiles to the remnant of our seed."—I Nephi 4:16.

Then Nephi added concerning his people, "They shall be grafted in, being a natural branch of the olive tree, into the true olive tree." All this would be part of "the restoration of the Jews, of the house of Israel" (verse 32). In time the cleavage between Jew and Gentile would be resolved. There would be one brotherhood with God the Father of all. This is God's design and intent. Nephi wrote of this with glowing spirit:

"Both shall be established in one; for there is one God and one Shepherd over all the earth. The time cometh that he shall manifest himself to all nations, to the Jews, and also to the Gentiles. And after he has manifested himself to the Jews and also to the Gentiles, then he shall manifest himself to the Gentiles, and also to the Jews."—I Nephi 3:196-199.

3. *Nations and peoples would rise or decline and fall on the basis of their own management, their own alignment with or separation from God.*

The Book of Mormon always places responsibility on persons and peoples. They are not puppets in the hands of

God, with their fortunes conditioned by the whims of God. There is no ordained schedule of happenings with men and nations subject to the whims of fate. The idea is noted that peoples and civilizations go through a cycle of life as do animals, with the eventuality of decline in old age and then death. It is implied that a people may continue living in prosperity and continuity if they live the way of rightness. This terse comment in I Nephi 5:128, 131, is the view of the Book of Mormon: "[God] raises up a righteous nation, and destroys the nations of the wicked. . . . And he loves those who will have him to be their God."

The Book of Mormon records the things that take place in the life of peoples. It is honest. It tells both sides, many sides. It speaks of people when they are riding high and when misfortune hits. It pictures how some peoples are on the way down—and out—when they think they are on top of everything.

The book carries a simple theology concerning the destiny of peoples. Those nations that line up with God survive. Those who go contrary to God's purpose decline and die. This does not take place at an instant, nor by decree of God, although this is the way many want God to work. This book sees the longtime sequence in what takes place.

The fortunes of peoples work out step by step. This applies to the building up and to the tearing down. Sometimes the final collapse might seem to come suddenly as an all-at-once catastrophe, as when the people are conquered by an invader. The Book of Mormon stresses how the seeds of disintegration have been working for a long, long while. This is the simple postulate: Wickedness leads to warfare and warfare leads to destruction.

Both destruction and continuance come in natural consequence. The Book of Mormon places the responsibility for both upon the peoples themselves. God designs and operates the universe so that it will hang together and continue. His way is the way of inclusive righteousness. This means that the total living matters. Lining up with one segmented factor in good living will not be enough. Full alignment is required. When people get off the right track and continue on detours and back roads, they decline and disintegrate. The consequences of natural law overtake them—the natural law of the universe that wickedness breeds eventual disaster.

God designs and calls certain groups to be his "chosen peoples." This is for mission in carrying out his purpose in the earth. Such a people must see what their mission is and qualify for carrying it out. There is no automatic favoritism. God never has any "teacher's pets." God grants special endowments to qualify a "chosen people" for the job they have to do with him and for him. If they do not carry out their assignment, they forfeit the right to this extra endowment. The Book of Mormon tells this kind of story. This way will continue among nations. They will come and go.

4. *The book of the Western land would come forth to support, to add witness to the book of the Eastern land.*

The Nephites took the keeping and the continuing of their scriptures most seriously. They saw what happened to peoples such as the Mulekites and the Lamanites who kept no record and used no scriptures. They believed that their record was to come forth in future years to both Jews and Gentiles. It would tell what happens to misbehaving peoples. It would be a second witness for Jesus Christ. It is identified as a "sealed" book that would require divine help in producing, in understanding. The coming forth of the book would be designated as "a marvelous work and a wonder" (II Nephi 11:147).

The reaction of religionists to the coming forth of the book was predicted. They would clutch to themselves their two-testaments Bible and would consider that a second book would be an intrusion on the Holy Bible. It would be viewed as sacrilegious to bring forth a second collection of scriptures, especially if the two collections were placed on the same level. The response of these religionists was stated this way, "A bible! A bible! We have a bible! There cannot be any more bible!" (II Nephi 12:45).

The homily of Nephi turns to the wide field of God's communion with men. He must not be confined to one book, to one land, to one people, to one language. A universal God would not be held to one set of writings, written and compiled in Judea. Nephi described God's outlook in these words:

> "Know you not that there are more nations than one? Know you not that I, the Lord your God, have created all man, and that I remember those who are upon the isles of the sea; and that . . . I bring forth my word to the children of men, even upon all the nations of the earth? Wherefore do you murmur because you shall receive more of my word? . . . I speak the same words to one nation as to another."—II Nephi 12:55-60.

The Book of Mormon eloquently affirms the multiple expression of God's communicating with his sons and daughters in many places. It speaks against the limiting monopoly of the Bible. The counsels of II Nephi 12:62-65 vision a continuing writing of scriptures with contributions from many men in many lands. What a wealth of scriptures are possible! This is the affirmation and outlook of the book: "I shall speak to all nations of the earth, and they shall write it" (verse 70).

5. *The Church of Christ would meet the opposition and undermining influence of "the great and abominable church"* (I Nephi 3:141). This term runs throughout the book. In the early days of the church there was inclination to consider this

the Roman Catholic Church. When we survey the entire Book of Mormon and bring together the several references to such a church the connotation seems more general, as if it points to whatever church forces exist that move away from God and deny the spirit and mission of the church of Christ. These qualities of such a church are noted: concern for wealth; opposition to and even destruction of "the saints of God" (I Nephi 3:144); alteration of scriptures and beliefs to suit its ends (I Nephi 3:170-172); prostitution of spirituality (I Nephi 3:225). Priestly position supersedes helpful ministry.

The affirmation is strong that in the long run such a church will go down (II Nephi 12:22). Always it carries the forces of disintegration within itself. It rises and declines in accordance with forces of renewal and recession within it. The conflict between forces for spiritual vision and forces for sham and sensuousness continue. Vigilance and vigor are ever needed to keep the right values and right dynamics to the fore. The Book of Mormon doctrine of "opposition in all things" applies here. There is no easy, let-things-go policy for the church of Christ. When ease and presumption abound, there is danger for the survival of the Church of God.

6. *God carries on his work with intent for longtime redemptive outreach to his people.*

This applies noticeably to the "lost sheep of the house of Israel." The group, led by Laman, revolted and divorced themselves from God. A thousand years later they killed off the Nephites. Then they turned on each other (Mormon 4:10). A millennium later the land was discovered by Gentiles from across the many waters. These Gentiles would overcome and make servile these descendants of Laman, but eventually the gospel of Jesus Christ would come to redeem these fallen peoples. What faith! What patience! What persistence! This was Nephi's summary of God's counsel to him. His seed and the seed of his brothers would be "destroyed and dwindle in unbelief" (I Nephi 3:185). Then "the book" and the gospel "would come forth from the Gentiles unto the remnant of the seed" of Nephi's brothers.

To date the Gentiles have not learned how to take up this project of ministering to the descendants of Laman now on the Western continent. And the sons of Laman have not learned how to respond. The Gentiles who have the book have to make the book come alive and learn how to share its living message with the descendants of those who survived at Cumorah a millennium and a half ago. The book affirms that God still has them on his heart.

7. *The evangelistic concern of God for all people continues; God calls his sons to live evangelistically with the other sheep, with all sheep.*

The oppressive happenings that closed out the Nephite story did not crush and bury the hope and sense of mission that was deep in Mormon. He wrote about what took place in the battle of Cumorah. He lamented that his people had got out of touch with God: "O ye fair ones, how could you have departed from the ways of the Lord!" (Mormon 3:18). Yet he did not surrender in spirit. He held to his conviction that the day would come when the people of his brothers would know God so they could live "in a state of happiness which has no end" (Mormon 3:29). He wrote to his son Moroni about faith and "sufficient hope."

Moroni focused on the eternal, universal Christ. This Christ was still saying what he had said to his disciples, "Go ye into all the world, and preach the gospel to every creature; he who believes and is baptized shall be saved" (Mormon 4:86). It took a man with a real sense of mission to say this when hopes seemed to have collapsed and countrymen had gone down in defeat and death.

The Christ of the Book of Mormon is ever saying what his

Father once said to him, that the Good Shepherd goes to every sheep in the world. This message stands out in the book: "I have other sheep. . . . I shall go to them. . . . They shall hear my voice and be numbered among my sheep, that there may be one fold and one shepherd."

This commission needs to be spoken in every language. Here let it be expressed in the language now spoken in the country where Land Bountiful lay. This can stand for many languages: "Tengo otras ovejas. . . . Vaya a ellas. . . . Ellas oirán mi voz, y serán contadas entre mis ovejas, para que haya un solo rebaño y un solo pastor" (Tercer Libro de Nephi 7:24, 26).

Today the Book of Mormon faces a world of three billion on our earth and millions of Amarinds (natives of America). The commission still sounds to believers to go out with convincing testimony that "Jesus is the Christ, the Eternal God, manifesting himself unto all nations." These words are credited to Mormon as he was closing out his written story. He ended his record on a note of faith that the story would continue, the story of the Shepherd and all his sheep.

Considerations for Conversation

1. Contrast "the end of time" and "the end of our age." What difference does this make about our conception of God, his program, and our part in this?

2. What does the term "latter day" mean to you today? The "latter day" of what? Do you see the "latter days" of one era moving forward into the "opening days" of another era?

3. How does the faith of Mormon and Moroni stand high in the light of what they endured in their closing days? What did they see God would be doing?

4. How did the Book of Mormon see the Gentiles and the Jews participating in God's longtime program? How did Mormon see Gentiles relating with his people and helping them?

5. In what place do you see the Book of Mormon in a world library of scriptures? What contribution can this book make to world religion, to world scriptures?

6. What is the outlook of the Book of Mormon toward "the rise and fall" of nations, of civilizations? What brings about the deterioration and collapse of peoples? Is a nation doomed to deterioration in time or may it continue as a healthy people? What is the outlook of the book for nations to come?

7. Why do you see the Book of Mormon writers speaking so strongly of "the great and abominable church"? With what do you see this descriptive phrase identified? What qualities made the great church so abominable? What warning was intended about what would take place in years to come?

8. Read in Church History, Volume I, page 180 ff. the identification of the Book of Mormon by Oliver Cowdery to the Delaware Indians early in 1831. Note the giving of a copy of the book. How would you make such a presentation to an Indian of South or North America today? What would you say about the mission of the book for them for future days?

9. How would you narrate the story of the "other sheep" to a friend in Asia or in Africa with the picture of "one fold and one shepherd"? How would you use the Book of Mormon's message about the "other sheep"? Would this suggest that there are some sheep that are not "others"?

10. How would you react if missionaries from non-English speaking cultures were to come to your area and call to the universal Christ? This happened in the Book of Mormon when Lamanites came to Nephites.

11. How do we go about translating the Book of Mormon into other languages? How might we miss the message and the mission? How is this bringing the book to other peoples in other languages essential to continuance of the story?

12. How do you see us as a church going about "manifesting" Jesus Christ to all nations? Contrast exhibiting Christ and broadcasting Christ. How do we consociate with persons and groups in order to manifest Christ? Our doing this continues the story.

Our Epilogue. Prologue for Today . . . The Christ of the Book lives with us in our times.

Recently a letter came to me concerning a brother in South America. He is a native son who had come into the Church of Jesus Christ during late months. He accepted the Book of Mormon as a work inspired by God. There was appeal in its application to his own land and its past. He accepted the book as dogma to be believed. Then he began to read, apply, and teach it. He lived the book; he caught its message. He met the Christ who had come in ancient times to his people. He wanted now to bring the living, universal Christ to others. This is what our missionary wrote:

"I wish you could meet Brother José. He has caught the vision of the Book of Mormon. He is making it live in our adult class here. He is making it live for them, because it is beginning to live in him. I thrill with great joy to see this happening in him and then through him in his brothers and sisters in South America."

This is what we are wanting to have happen in all of us. We are needing to see with larger vision the intent of God to reveal himself to all peoples, then and now. We are needing to see how this revelation comes to each people in the meaningful, functional terms of their culture and needs. We can see what happens in people as they turn away from and as they turn to God. We can see what miracles take place as persons are transformed and become God's sons and daughters. Our lives can be enriched as we live with these noble characters.

Let's get inside the book, as José has done. Let's let it live in us! The contagion of such living will carry it to others.